# COMMUNICATING
# WITH
# CONFIDENCE

CAMBRIDGE ADULT EDUCATION
A Division of Simon & Schuster
Upper Saddle River, New Jersey

*Executive Editor:* Mark Moscowitz
*Project Editors:* Laura Baselice, Lynn W. Kloss, Robert McIlwaine
*Writer:* Theresa Flynn-Nason
*Production Manager:* Penny Gibson
*Production Editor:* Nicole Cypher
*Marketing Manager:* Will Jarred
*Interior Electronic Design:* Mimi Raihl
*Illustrator:* Allen Davis
*Photo Research:* Jenifer Hixson
*Electronic Page Production:* Mimi Raihl
*Cover Design:* Mimi Raihl

Printed in the United States of America.

1 2 3 4 5 6 7 8 9 10  99 98 97 96 95

ISBN: 0-8359-4671-1

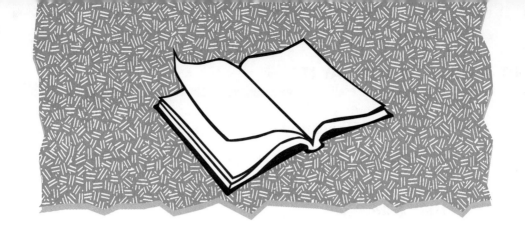

# CONTENTS

# Getting the Message Across

## In this unit you will:

- understand what is needed for communication to happen.
- think about why people communicate.
- learn healthy communication skills.

## Key Words

**communication:** the sharing of ideas
**message:** an idea or information
**interpret:** to explain the meaning of something
**goal:** purpose
**positive:** healthy
**negative:** harmful

## Meet José Montoya and Lisa Maldonado

José Montoya and Lisa Maldonado had been going out for six months. They got along well. They liked being with one another.

Then Lisa began to think about their relationship. She wanted to know where it was heading. She knew that José was the one for her. She wanted to make some kind of commitment. But she was not sure that José was ready to take that step.

Lisa wanted to talk to José about her feelings. But she was worried about what he would think. José might feel as if she was pressuring him. He might feel that she was trying to pin him down.

Lisa had two choices. She could just let things keep going the way they were. Or she could tell José how she felt.

Lisa decided to talk to José. She thought about what she wanted to say to him. She decided to keep it simple. She would just be honest, and say what she felt.

One Saturday, Lisa and José were at the park. Lisa decided to have the talk.

"José, I have something I want to talk to you about," Lisa said.

José looked at her. "Sure," he said. "What's up?"

"I've been thinking about us a lot lately," said Lisa. "I'm not really sure about the relationship."

José looked surprised. "What's wrong?" he asked. "Don't you want to go out anymore?"

"Of course I do," replied Lisa. "I'm very happy being with you. You're really special to me."

"Then what's the problem?" said José.

"It's just that I'm not sure where we are headed. I don't want just to go out with you for the rest of my life," continued Lisa.

"Well, what *do* you want?" asked José.

Lisa took a deep breath. "I'd like us to make some kind of commitment," she says.

"I'm not ready to get married," José responded.

"I'm not talking about marriage," said Lisa. "Maybe someday, but not now. I was thinking about not dating anyone else. I'd agree to that. What about you?"

José thought for a moment. "I haven't seen anyone else since we started dating. I could keep it that way." he said.

Lisa smiled. "I'm really glad we had this talk," she said. "I feel much better!"

## Think About It

Circle the answer to each question. (Check your answers on page 119.)

1. What did Lisa want to tell José?
   a. She is dating someone else.
   b. She doesn't want to see him anymore.
   c. She wants to make some kind of commitment.

2. What did José and Lisa agree to do?
   a. Not date other people
   b. Get married
   c. Move in together

## The Three Parts of Communication

**Communication** is the sharing of ideas. When José Montoya and Lisa Maldonado talked, they shared their ideas. They communicated with one another.

Every day of your life, you communicate with others. Your communication takes many forms. However, all kinds of communication have three parts. These three things are needed for communication to happen.

## Who Sends the Message?

The first thing that's needed is a sender. The sender starts the communication. The sender begins the exchange of ideas.

Lisa was the sender of the communication between herself and José. She started their talk. Her actions began an exchange of ideas.

The second thing that's needed for communication is a message. A **message** is an idea or information. It's what the sender wants to share with another person.

### Think About It

Circle the sentence that states the message Lisa wanted to send to José. (Check your answers on page 119.)

1. "I want to date other people."

2. "I don't want to marry you."

3. "I want us to make some kind of commitment to each other."

# Different Kinds of Messages

Most messages are made up of spoken words. Sometimes the words are written, not spoken. However, not all messages are made up of words. Actions can also send a message. A smile sends the message that someone is happy or pleased. A frown sends the opposite message.

A sign is another way of sending a message. Signs posted along a highway send messages to drivers. For example, the number on a speed limit sign tells drivers how fast they can go.

Messages are also sent by symbols. A symbol is an object that stands for something else. A cross is a symbol. It has a specific religious message. A heart is another type of symbol. It sends a message of love.

## Think About It

Listed below are things that send a message without words. Decide what message is sent by each item listed. Write the message in the space provided. (Check your answers on page 119.)

1. A handshake

2. A green light on a traffic light

3. A street sign that shows children walking

4. Pointing your thumb upward

5. A gold band worn on the ring finger of a person's left hand

# Who Gets the Message?

You have learned that communication needs a sender and a message. But there is one more thing needed for communication to happen: There must be a receiver. The receiver gets the message. The receiver must then **interpret** or explain the meaning of the message.

Most people think that the message a receiver gets can only be in words. Often, that is true. But not all messages are made up of words. The receiver must sometimes interpret an action, a sign, or a symbol. In the last activity, you were the receiver. You had to interpret the meaning of each message listed. You received messages that were sent without words.

## Check What You've Learned

You have learned that communication involves a sender, a message, and a receiver. Listed below are different kinds of communication. Name the sender, the message, and the receiver in each example. (Check your answers on page 119.)

1. Gaynelle left a note for her husband on the kitchen table. It said, "I went to the post office."

   Sender:

   Message:

   Receiver:

2. Masako stood up and clapped at the end of a concert.

   Sender:

   Message:

   Receiver:

3. In the middle of a basketball game, Ali looked toward the referee and put his hands in the shape of the letter T.

   Sender:

   Message:

   Receiver:

**4.** An advertisement in a magazine shows a beautiful young woman smoking a certain brand of cigarettes.

Sender:

Message:

Receiver:

**5.** Tom yawned as his wife told him about her day at work.

Sender:

Message:

Receiver:

**6.** Dawn's counselor reached out and patted Dawn's hand as she spoke.

Sender:

Message:

Receiver:

**7.** Alicia heard her son laugh as he watched a cartoon.

Sender:

Message:

Receiver:

**8.** Bill's parole officer stood with his arms crossed and frowned at Bill.

Sender:

Message:

Receiver:

Read each statement. If the statement is true, write T on the answer blank. If the statement is false, write F on the answer blank.

_____ **9.** Communication needs a sender, a message, and a receiver.

_____ **10.** Communication starts with a sender.

_____ **11.** All messages have words.

_____ **12.** A receiver interprets a message.

_____ **13.** It is impossible to receive a message that has no words.

# LESSON 2

## Why Do People Communicate?

You have just discovered what is needed for communication: a sender, a message, and a receiver. Now it is time to think about why you need to communicate.

Every time you communicate you have a goal. A **goal** is a purpose. It is what you hope to achieve. Your communication goal is the idea or information that you want to share with someone else.

Remember Lisa Maldonado? She had a communication goal. She wanted José to understand her feelings. Lisa wanted José to know that she needed some kind of commitment.

Before Lisa talked to José, she identified her communication goal. She thought about what she would say. Then she chose the words she would use to get her message across to José.

You also have a goal in mind whenever you communicate. You probably don't think as much about your communication goal as Lisa did. Whether you realize it or not, your communications always have some kind of purpose.

## Communication Goals

You communicate with many different people. You communicate with family members. You communicate with friends. You communicate at work.

You communicate for many different reasons. You might tell a family member how you feel about something. You might speak with a friend about plans for the evening. You might talk with people at work about the job.

Every communication is special. However, there are six common communication goals. Most of your communications have one of these goals. They are:

- To let someone know how you feel
- To get to know someone
- To teach or share information
- To learn
- To entertain or have fun
- To solve a problem

Think about Lisa. Her communication goal was to let someone know how she felt. She wanted José to know that she needed some kind of commitment from him. This communication goal was the reason she spoke to José. It was what she hoped to achieve.

## Check What You've Learned _____

Look at the list of common communication goals above. Read the sentences below. Name the goal of each communication described. Write the goal in the space provided. (Check your answers on page 119.)

1. Ed said "Hi" to his new neighbor. Then he shook the woman's hand.

   Communication goal:

2. Maria looked at the speed limit sign posted on the highway.

   Communication goal:

3. Marci laughed at the TV show.

   Communication goal:

4. Omar asked a police officer how to get to Main Street.

   Communication goal:

5. Juan showed Pat how to use the washing machine.

   Communication goal:

6. Rochelle began to cry at a going-away party for her friend.

   Communication goal:

## What About You?

Write the answer to the following questions in the space provided.

1.  Think about the last phone call you made. What was your communication goal?

2.  Think about the last thing that you wrote. What was your communication goal?

3.  Think about the last talk you had. What was your communication goal?

## Check What You've Learned

Read each statement. If the statement is true, write T on the answer blank. If the statement is false, write F on the answer blank. (Check your answers on page 119.)

\_\_\_\_\_ **1.** A goal is a purpose.

\_\_\_\_\_ **2.** All communications have the same goal.

\_\_\_\_\_ **3.** You communicate in order to achieve a goal.

## Healthy Communication

You communicate for a specific purpose. You have a goal. You know the message that you want to share with another person.

## Positive Communication

Communication is healthy when you reach your goals in a **positive**, or healthy, way. The communication between Lisa Maldonado and José Montoya was healthy. This did not happen by accident. Lisa did certain things to make sure that the communication was positive.

First, Lisa identified her communication goal. She knew her purpose. She knew what she wanted to achieve.

Lisa thought about what she would say to José. She chose her words carefully. She made sure that her words sent a clear message to José.

Lisa was honest. She told José exactly how she felt. She did not lie. She did not accuse José. She did not speak in a harsh way. She did not show anger toward him.

Lisa spoke to José in a respectful way. Her words showed that she valued José.

Lisa kept the communication positive. This helped José listen to her message. It made it easier for José to understand her ideas.

## Negative Communication

Lisa could have tried to achieve her communication goal in other ways. She could have yelled at José. She could have called him names. She could have lied to him.

These **negative**, or harmful, things would have stopped the communication. They would have caused José to stop listening. Lisa would not have achieved her communication goal.

## What About You?

Think about a time when someone yelled at you. Answer these questions about that communication. Write your answers in the space provided.

1. What did the sender say to you?

2. How did the words make you feel?

3. Do you think the sender achieved his or her communication goal? Explain why.

## Think About It

Read each pair of statements. Circle the statement that is an example of positive communication. (Check your answers on page 119.)

1. "I don't know what you are talking about!"

   "Could you explain that again?"

2. "I need to be on time for my appointment."

   "I'm not going to let you make me late again."

3. "Do you think I could choose what we will do today?"

   "You never let me decide how we'll spend the day."

4. "Could you let me pass?"

   "Get out of my way!"

5. "You're going too fast."

   "Could you slow down a little?"

6. "I'd like to do something different today."

   "I'm sick of doing the same old thing."

7. "I'd love to hear how you feel about this."

   "You never tell me how you feel."

8. "What's wrong with you?"

   "Is everything OK?"

# Unit 1 Review

## In this unit:

- You learned that communication is the sharing of ideas. For communication to happen, there must be a sender, a message, and a receiver.

- You discovered that you communicate to achieve a goal. The most common communication goals are to let someone know how you feel, to get to know someone, to teach or share information, to learn, to entertain or have fun, and to solve a problem.

- You learned that communication is healthy when it helps you reach goals in a positive way. Knowing your communication goal, carefully choosing your words, being honest, and treating others with respect keep communication positive.

# Key Words

Match each word in Column A with the correct meaning in Column B. Write the letter from Column B on the answer blank in Column A. (Check your answers on page 119.)

**Column A**

_____ 1. communication

_____ 2. goal

_____ 3. interpret

_____ 4. message

_____ 5. negative

_____ 6. positive

**Column B**

**a.** to explain the meaning of a message

**b.** healthy

**c.** the sharing of ideas

**d.** purpose

**e.** an idea or information

**f.** harmful

# Key Ideas

Write the answer to each question in the space provided. (Check your answers on page 119.)

1. What three things are needed for communication to happen?

2. What are two ways to send a message without words?

3. Why do people communicate?

4. What are three things you can do to keep communication positive?

5. How do negative practices stop communication from happening?

# What About You?

Think about what you have learned in Unit 1. What information do you plan to use in your daily life? Explain.

# A Matter of Style

## In this unit you will:

- learn what makes up a communication style.
- find out how communication styles affect communication.
- discover why people have different communication styles.

# Meet Dave Jenkins

Dave Jenkins is assigned to a community service program. He must spend 20 hours each week working in a neighborhood cleanup program. Dave doesn't mind the work. It helps to keep him busy. It helps him stay out of trouble.

Every Monday, Dave reports to the program supervisor. She gives Dave a job for the week. One week, Dave's job was cleaning up the flower gardens around the library.

Dave got right to work. He liked working outdoors. He liked the fresh air and sunshine. He also liked working with plants. When he was a child, his family had kept a vegetable garden. Dave had helped care for the plants.

But that was a long time ago. Things had not worked out as Dave had planned. Since then, the closest he had come to gardening was cleaning up the library's garden.

Dave worked slowly. He didn't use the rake the supervisor had given him. Instead, he got down on his hands and knees. With his hands, he carefully moved dead leaves away from the plants. Then he pulled out the weeds. Dave was very careful not to harm the plants.

Dave worked steadily. He didn't stop for a minute. After two hours, he had cleared out a small part of the garden. Suddenly, he heard the supervisor call his name.

"Dave," she yelled. "What are you doing?"

Dave turned around. The supervisor was standing in a spot that Dave had just cleared out. Her right foot crushed a plant. This made Dave angry. He had been so careful not to harm a single plant.

"I'm doing what you told me to do." Dave answered angrily.

"That's not what I told you," she said. "I told you to use the rake. You'll never get anything done on your hands and knees. You're just wasting time."

Dave felt anger growing inside him. She didn't know what she was talking about. She didn't know as much about plants as he did. But she was giving the orders.

Something snapped inside Dave. He jumped up. "You think you know everything," he shouted.

The supervisor shook her finger at Dave. "I should have known better than to give you this job. Give the rake to Al. He'll finish the garden. I'm giving you a different job."

Dave threw the rake across the garden. "I'm done for today," he said. As the supervisor called after him, Dave walked down the block.

## Think About It

Do you think Dave and his supervisor communicated in a healthy manner? Explain. (Check your answer on page 119.)

# LESSON 4

## What Is a Communication Style?

Dave and his supervisor had problems communicating. They did not get their messages across to one another. Why? Their communication styles got in the way.

## The Power of Style

A communication style is how a person sends messages to others. Four things make up a communication style. They are:

1. Your tone of voice
2. Your background
3. Your body movements and gestures
4. The words you use

Communication styles are powerful. A positive communication style helps listeners get the right message. A negative communication style can give listeners the wrong message.

In Unit 1 you learned what is needed for communication to happen. You also learned why you communicate. Now you need to think about the *way* that you communicate. You need to think about your communication style. You must work to develop a positive communication style. This will help you get your ideas across to others.

## Think About It

It's time to start thinking about your communication style. Complete each of the following statements in a way that describes you. Write your answers in the space provided.

1. I smile to show people that I

**2.** I frown to show people that I


**3.** I put my hands on my hips to show people that I


**4.** I stare at a person to show that I


**5.** I point at a person to show that I


**6.** I speak in a loud voice to show people that I


**7.** I speak in a soft voice to show people that I


Now think about how another person's communication style makes you feel. Complete each of the following statements in a way that describes your feelings. Write your answers in the space provided.

**8.** When someone points at me, I feel


**9.** When someone speaks to me in a loud voice, I feel


**10.** When someone speaks to me in a soft voice, I feel


**11.** When someone smiles at me, I feel


**12.** When someone stares at me, I feel

# LESSON 5

## Tone of Voice

Think about all the different ways that you speak. Sometimes, you talk softly. Sometimes, you speak loudly. Sometimes, you speak with a lot of energy. Other times, you speak in a bored or dull manner.

Your voice has different sounds. The sound of your voice is its tone. Tone of voice sends a message to a listener. It can help the listener hear your words. Or it can keep the listener from hearing your message.

## Negative Tone

The tone of voice used by Dave Jenkins's supervisor harmed their communication. When she said, "What are you doing?" she spoke loudly. Her words sounded angry. Dave heard the tone. He got the message that she was mad at him. He got the message that he had done something wrong. This message made Dave angry. Their communication became negative.

## Positive Tone

Dave's supervisor might have used a different tone of voice. She could have said the same words in an even tone. She could have said the words more like a question. This would have given Dave a different message. He would have heard that she was interested in him. He would have heard that she wanted to learn more about what he was doing. A light tone of voice would have made Dave feel respected. Their communication would have been positive.

Say each of the following sentences in two different ways. Listen to yourself. Hear the messages your tone of voice sends out.

1. "I'd like to do that!"

2. "What do you want?"

3. "Do you know what to do?"

4. "What's the problem?"

5. "Why should I go?"

# Matching Messages and Tones

You send a message with the words you say. You send another message with the sound of your voice. It is important that the messages match. If not, the listener hears two different things. The listener gets confused. The listener doesn't know which message to believe.

Suppose someone said told you, "I'm glad to see you" in an angry voice. You would hear two different messages. The words would tell you that you are valuable and respected. But the speaker's tone of voice would tell you that the speaker is angry. You would be confused. You wouldn't know which message to believe. Communication would stop.

If the speaker told you, "I'm glad to see you" in a light, happy tone, you'd hear one message. This is because the tone would match the words. The sound of the speaker's voice would support the words. The tone would make the words believable. The message would be clear to you.

You should think about your tone of voice when communicating with others. Be sure that your tone matches your words. If you are saying something important, use a serious tone. If you are saying something for fun, use a light tone. If you are telling someone how you feel, use a sincere tone. Matching your tone to your words will help you communicate with others.

(Check your answers on page 119.)

1. Suppose someone said, "I love you" in a dull, bored voice. What message would you get from the speaker's words?

2. What message would you get from the speaker's tone of voice?

# Watch Out For Emotions

Emotions can also get in the way of communications. **Emotions** are strong feelings such as anger or disgust. These strong feelings interfere with your thoughts.

Emotions got in the way of Dave's communication with his supervisor. Dave was angry with his supervisor. His anger made him say and do things he wouldn't normally do. Dave's emotions stopped their communication.

What could Dave have done to keep the communication healthy? He could have waited to speak to his supervisor. He might have asked, "Could I have a minute to myself, please?" This would have given Dave time to calm down. He could have gotten his anger under control. Then, when he was ready, he could have continued their communication.

Strong emotions also affect the listener. A listener can feel the sender's anger. This causes the listener to withdraw or step back from the communication. The listener stops hearing the sender's message.

## Check What You've Learned

Read each statement. If the statement is true, write T on the answer blank. If the statement is false, write F on the answer blank. (Check your answers on page 119.)

_____ 1. Your voice always sounds the same.

_____ 2. A speaker's tone of voice sends a message to a listener.

_____ 3. Strong emotions help a listener hear a sender's message.

## Different Backgrounds and Communication

Every day you communicate with many people. They are different from you. They have different families. They have different friends. They spend their days doing different things. They live different lives.

These differences affect communication. Your life experiences determine how you send messages to others. Your life experiences determine how you interpret messages sent to you.

Suppose you are at a friend's party. At the end of the party, your host walks you to the door. When saying good-bye, your host kisses you on the cheek. How would this action make you feel?

That all depends on your life experiences. For some people, a good-bye kiss is a common act. It sends a message of caring and affection. For other people, a good-bye kiss is unusual. These people would probably be shocked by the act. It would make them feel uncomfortable.

### What About You?

1. How would *you* feel if your host gave you a kiss on the cheek?

2. Describe the message you would receive.

# A Good Communicator

A good communicator gets his or her message across to others. A good communicator thinks about the receiver. A good communicator makes sure to send a message in a way that the receiver will understand.

Being a good communicator takes time. It takes effort. It takes patience.

In order to be a good communicator, you need to learn about others. You need to show that you value people who are different from you. You must show respect for the receiver. This will help you get your message across.

## What About You?

Think about how you communicate with people who are different from you. Then read each statement. Circle the number that *best* describes you.

1. I think about the different ways that people communicate.

| 5 | 4 | 3 | 2 | 1 |
|---|---|---|---|---|
| Always | | Sometimes | | Never |

2. I try to learn how other people communicate.

| 5 | 4 | 3 | 2 | 1 |
|---|---|---|---|---|
| Always | | Sometimes | | Never |

3. I think about how I can send a clear message to others.

| 5 | 4 | 3 | 2 | 1 |
|---|---|---|---|---|
| Always | | Sometimes | | Never |

4. I treat people who are different from me in a respectful way.

| 5 | 4 | 3 | 2 | 1 |
|---|---|---|---|---|
| Always | | Sometimes | | Never |

5. If someone doesn't understand me, I try to send the message another way.

| 5 | 4 | 3 | 2 | 1 |
|---|---|---|---|---|
| Always | | Sometimes | | Never |

6. I like communicating with people who are different from me.

| 5 | 4 | 3 | 2 | 1 |
|---|---|---|---|---|
| Always | | Sometimes | | Never |

7. I am patient when a person doesn't understand my message.

| 5 | 4 | 3 | 2 | 1 |
|---|---|---|---|---|
| Always | | Sometimes | | Never |

Add up the numbers you circled and check your score on the chart below.

| Score | Meaning |
|---|---|
| 28–35 | You have good communication skills. |
| 18–27 | You are an average communicator. |
| 7–17 | You need to work on your communication skills. |

# Communication Differences

There are some things you should think of when communicating with others. They are eye contact, personal space, being direct, and time.

**Eye Contact.** Eye contact means looking at a speaker's face when he or she is talking. In the United States, listeners usually make eye contact with a speaker. This shows that the listener is paying attention. It shows that the listener respects the speaker.

People from other countries have a different opinion of eye contact. In some places, people think that it is disrespectful to look directly at a speaker. For these people, a listener shows that he or she honors the speaker by looking away.

## What About You?

How do you feel when a person looks directly at you?

**Personal Space.** Personal space refers to the distance you keep between yourself and others. Some people need a lot of personal space. They don't like others coming too close to them. It makes them feel uncomfortable.

Other people need less personal space. They are comfortable when another person stands right next to them. These people don't like a wide distance between themselves and others.

## What About You?

How do you feel when a person stands close to you?

**Being Direct.** Some people like to say exactly what they think. This is common in the United States. We believe in free speech. We believe that all people have the right to say what they think.

Suppose you wanted a friend to help you with something. You might say, "Give me a hand with this." You would tell your friend exactly what you needed. You would be direct.

Some people feel that it is rude to speak directly. They would not say exactly what they feel or want. To them, it would be very disrespectful to speak directly. Such people might say, "If you have a minute, would help with this?" If you are used to speaking directly, this would give you a mixed message. You might think that the person really did not need help . You might think that the person didn't care whether or not you helped.

## What About You?

Suppose a friend said, "I have some leftover pasta. It wouldn't bother me if you ate it." How would you interpret this message?

**Time.** Some people feel that it is important to be on time. To them, being late is a sign of disrespect. To them, tardiness sends a message that you don't value other people.

Some people do not have this view of time. They feel that it is normal to be late. They don't see lateness as disrespectful. They don't get a negative message when someone is late.

## Check What You've Learned

Read each statement. If the statement is true, write T on the answer blank. If the statement if false, write F on the answer blank. (Check your answers on page 119.)

_____ 1. Your background affects how you send and receive messages.

_____ 2. Learning about others helps you be a good communicator.

_____ 3. A good communicator understands that people communicate in different ways.

_____ 4. All people think that it is rude to look away from a speaker.

_____ 5. Everyone needs the same amount of personal space.

# Unit 2 Review

## In this unit:

- You learned that the way you send messages to others is your communication style. The four things that make up your communication style are your tone of voice, your background, your body movements and gestures, and your words.

- You discovered that your tone of voice sends a message to listeners. Matching your tone of voice to your words helps a listener interpret your message.

- You learned that a good communicator knows that people are different. A good communicator works to learn about these differences. A good communicator uses this information to send clear messages to others.

## Key Word

(Check your answer on page 119.)

What are emotions?

## Key Ideas

Write the answer to each question in the space provided. (Check your answers on page 119.)

1. What four things make up your communication style?

**2.** How does tone of voice affect communication?

**3.** Name three traits of a good communicator.

**4.** What are some things you should think about when speaking to someone who is different from you?

**5.** Why are some people uncomfortable making eye contact with a speaker?

## What About You? _____

Explain how working through Unit 2 has helped you become a good communicator.

# Real World Connection

## The Job Interview

Gian walked nervously into the office. The woman sitting behind the counter looked up. "May I help you?" she asked.

"I have an **appointment** with Mrs. Will," Gian answered.

The woman looked at a book on the counter. "What's your name?" the woman asked.

"Gian Chung," he replied.

"Yes, Mrs. Will is expecting you. But she's running a bit late. Please sit down over there. I'll call you when she's ready."

Gian sat in a **comfortable** chair. He wondered what questions Mrs. Will would ask him. He wondered what he would say.

Gian really wanted to jump up and run out of the room. He needed the job. He needed the money badly.

Finally, the woman behind the counter called his name. "Mrs. Will is ready for you now," she said.

As Gian entered the room, Mrs. Will came toward him. Shaking his hand, she said, "I'm Mrs. Will. Thanks for coming in, Mr. Chung. Why not sit in that chair and we can talk?"

Gian sat. He was so nervous he could hardly speak. He looked down at his shoes.

"So, you're **applying** for the opening in our nighttime cleaning **crew**. Have you ever done this kind of work before?"

Gian thought for a moment. "I used to be in charge of keeping the equipment clean at my last job," he replied. "I also do all the cleaning in my apartment," he added.

Mrs. Will smiled. "Good. Well, can you tell me why you want this job?" she asked.

Gian kept looking at his shoes. He didn't know what to say. He kept silent.

"Mr. Chung, is something wrong?" she asked.

Finally, Gian looked up. "Oh, I really want the job," he **blurted**.

"Well, what is the problem? You are hardly talking to me. All you do is **stare** at the floor!" said Mrs. Will.

Gian was surprised. How could she think he didn't want the job?

"I'm sorry," he said. "I guess I'm just a little nervous."

"OK," said Mrs. Will. "Let's start over again. Why don't you tell me a little about yourself."

Gian took a deep breath. He told her about other places where he had worked. He explained why he had left each job.

Mrs. Will listened carefully. When he had finished speaking, she said, "Now tell me why I should hire you."

Gian thought. After a few moments he looked up at her. "I'd be a good worker," he said. "You could **depend** on me."

Mrs. Will glanced at her watch. "That's the kind of worker I need," she said. "Call my secretary tomorrow. She'll let you know if you have the job."

Gian stood up. He shook Mrs. Will's outstretched hand. "Thanks," he mumbled.

Gian was proud of himself. He could have run out of the office. But he didn't. Even though it was scary, he had made himself stay for the interview. He had been brave enough to try and get the job.

## Key Words

In the story, eight words are in **bold print.** These words are listed below. Circle the correct meaning for each word. If you have trouble, go back and read the sentence containing the word. Look for clues in the sentence. Use the clues to figure out the meaning of the word. (Check your answers on page 120.)

1. **Appointment** means
   a. job.
   b. meeting.
   c. office.
   d. secretary.

2. **Comfortable** means
   a. painful.
   b. wooden.
   c. giving a bad feeling.
   d. giving a good feeling.

3. **Applying** means
   a. seeking.
   b. working.
   c. leaving.
   d. finding.

4. **Crew** means
   a. person.
   b. ship.
   c. group of chairs.
   d. group of people.

5. **Blurted** means
   a. yelled.
   b. said suddenly
   c. said quietly.
   d. thought.

6. **Stare** means
   a. stood.
   b. sat.
   c. walked.
   d. looked.

7. **Depend** means
   a. rely on.
   b. let go.
   c. call on.
   d. go to.

8. **Skipped** means
   a. made.
   b. went to.
   c. planned.
   d. missed.

## Check What You've Learned

Circle the letter of the best answer to each question. (Check your answers on page 120.)

1. How did Gian feel when he walked into the office?
   a. Proud
   b. Happy
   c. Nervous
   d. Sick

2. While Gian waited in the office, he
   a. read a book.
   b. listened to the radio.
   c. talked to the secretary.
   d. was nervous.

3. What kind of job was Gian applying for?
   a. Secretary
   b. Cleaning crew member
   c. Cook
   d. Chair maker

4. During the interview, Gian stared at
   a. a magazine.
   b. the secretary.
   c. Mrs. Will.
   d. his shoes.

5. Mrs. Will thought that Gian
   a. didn't want the job.
   b. would be a good boss.
   c. couldn't read.
   d. would be a good secretary.

6. Gian told Mrs. Will that she should hire him because he
   a. would work for low wages.
   b. had lots of experience.
   c. was dependable.
   d. was strong.

7. When Gian left the interview, he felt
   a. worried.
   b. proud.
   c. angry.
   d. nervous.

8. If Gian does not get the job, he will
   a. try for another job.
   b. go to school.
   c. move to a different city.
   d. call his old boss.

## Think About It

Write the answer to each question in the space provided. (Check your answer on page 120.)

1. In Unit 2 you learned about eye contact. What message did Gian's eye contact send to Mrs. Will?

2. Do you think that Gian and Mrs. Will had the same communication style? Explain.

# UNIT **3**

# You Can't Hear It

## In this unit you will:

- learn about body language.
- think about the messages that you send with your body.
- discover how body language can help you communicate.

## Key Word

**body language:** the messages that your body sends to others

# Meet Mia Burke and Ling Chen

Mia Burke struggled up the stairs. Her apartment was on the fourth floor. That meant four sets of stairs.

She held the baby tightly in one arm. Her other arm was wrapped around a heavy shopping bag. Her arms felt as though they might break off.

Finally, Mia reached her apartment. She put the baby in her crib. She put the bag on a table. Then Mia sat down. She needed to rest a minute.

Just then the doorbell rang. Mia moaned. "Why doesn't everyone leave me alone?" she thought. Angrily, Mia went to the door. She opened it quickly.

A woman about Mia's age stood at the door. Mia had never seen her before. "Yes," said Mia in an irritated voice. "What do you want?"

The stranger looked uncomfortable. Quietly she said, "I want to introduce myself. My name is Ling Chen. I just moved in next door."

Mia thrust her hand out the door. "I'm Mia Burke," she said. She roughly shook the woman's hand. In an even voice, Mia said "I'm glad to meet you."

Ling just stood there. "What does she want?" Mia wondered. Neither woman spoke. Finally, Mia said, "I've got to go now. I'm really busy." With that, she closed the door.

## Think About It _____

Circle the word that answers the question. (Check your answers on page 120.)

1.  What word best describes Mia?

    Kind          Helpful          Angry

2.  What word best describes Ling?

    Tired          Uncomfortable          Mad

# LESSON 7

## Communicating Without Words

You just read about the communication between Mia Burke and Ling Chen. The women used words to send messages. But they also communicated in other ways.

In Unit 2 you learned about tone of voice. Mia's tone of voice sent a message to Ling. When Mia said, "What do you want?" the tone of her voice was angry. The sound of Mia's voice told Ling that she was mad.

Then Mia said, "I'm glad to meet you" in an even voice. Ling heard the sound of her voice. It sent her a message. It said that Mia was really *not* glad to meet her.

## Think About It

Suppose you were Ling. What would you think of Mia? Explain your feelings in the space provided. (Check your answers on page 120.)

## Body Language

Mia and Ling sent messages in other ways. They also communicated with body language.

**Body language** is the messages that your body sends to others. Mia sent Ling a message when she opened the door quickly. The sudden action showed that Mia was annoyed.

Mia sent Ling another message when she thrust her hand toward Ling. The action was quick. It told Ling that Mia did not have time for her. It made Ling feel unwelcome.

The rough handshake sent yet another message. It showed that Mia was mad. It said that Ling was bothering Mia.

Ling received all these messages. She interpreted them. They told her "Go away! I don't like you!"

## Think About It

Did Mia's body language help or hurt the communication? Explain in the space provided. (Check your answer on page 120.)

# The Importance of Body Language

Body language is an important part of your communication style. The way you sit, stand, and use your hands sends messages to others. These messages are powerful. Many times, listeners "hear" your body language messages more than your word messages.

Good communicators use body language to get their message across. They match their body language with their words. This helps to send a clear message to others.

If you want to be a good communicator, you need to think about your body language. You need to use positive body language. You need to avoid negative body language. Doing so will help you reach your communication goals.

## Check What You've Learned

Read each statement. If the statement is true, write T on the answer blank. If the statement is false, write F on the answer blank. (Check your answers on page 120.)

____ 1. The way you stand sends a message to others.

____ 2. Messages you send with your body are hard to understand.

____ 3. A good communicator does not think about body language.

____ 4. Your body language should match your words.

____ 5. Positive body language helps you reach your communication goal.

## What's the Message?

Think again about the communication between Mia Burke and Ling Chen. Ling said very little. She spoke only when she had to. When she did talk, Ling used a soft tone of voice.

Why did Ling act this way? She was reacting to Mia's body language. Ling received a message from Mia. She "heard" that Mia was mad. She "heard" that Mia was annoyed. Ling interpreted this message. She thought that Mia did not like her. Ling felt unwanted. She felt uncomfortable. Ling reacted by being very quiet.

Ling's body language sent a message to Mia. Mia "heard" that Ling was bored with her. Mia thought that Ling's quietness was a sign of indifference. She figured that Ling really *didn't* want to be friends with her.

But that was not what Ling really felt. What happened between the two women shows an important part of body language. An action does not mean the same thing to everyone. An action can be interpreted in different ways.

You cannot always know how a listener will interpret your body language. But you can make some good guesses. How? By first thinking about how *you* would interpret certain actions.

## Think About It

Listed below are different actions. Think about the message you receive when you see a person do each action. Write the message in the space provided. (Check your answers on page 120.)

**1.** When I see someone smile, I get the message

2. When I see someone frown, I get the message

3. When I see someone jump up and down, I get the message

4. When someone points at me, I get the message

5. When I see someone yawn, I get the message

6. When someone shakes my hand roughly, I get the message

7. When I see someone standing with his arms crossed in front of his chest, I get the message

8. When I see someone slumped down low in a chair, I get the message

9. When someone winks at me, I get the message

10. When someone stares at me, I get the message

11. When I see someone put her hands on her hips, I get the message

12. When someone shakes a fist at me, I get the message

Listed below are different kinds of messages. Think about the body language *you* use to send each message. Describe your body language in the space provided.

**1.** I show others that I am happy by

**2.** I show others that I am sad by

**3.** I show others that I am worried by

**4.** I show others that I am angry by

**5.** I show others that I am listening to them by

**6.** I show others that I am bored by

**7.** I show others that I care about them by

**8.** I show others that I am determined by

**9.** I show others that I am unsure by

**10.** I show others that I am confident by

## Match Your Body Language With Your Words

You have learned that body language sends a message to listeners. Your words also send a message to listeners. A good communicator makes sure that these two messages are the same. How? Good communicators match their body language with their words.

Suppose you met a new neighbor. She said, "I really want to get to know you." But, as she spoke these words, she looked over your shoulder at someone else.

How would you feel? Probably confused. Her words sent one message. But her body language sent a totally different message. Her communication was unclear.

Now, if the person looked directly at you and said the same words, you'd get a clear message. You'd know that the person meant what she said. You'd believe her.

It is important that your body language match your words. If it does not, the listener will be confused. The listener will not believe or trust you. The communication will not be effective.

## Check What You've Learned

Read each statement. If the statement is true, write T on the answer blank. If the statement is false, write F on the answer blank. (Check your answers on page 120.)

____ 1. A certain kind of body language means the same thing to all listeners.

____ 2. A good communicator matches body language with words.

____ 3. A listener is more likely to believe a speaker if the speaker's body language and words match.

## What About You?

Think about the last time a person said something nice to you. Did the person's body language match his or her words? Did you "hear" a clear message? Write your answers in the space provided.

# LESSON 9

## Helpful or Harmful Body Language?

You have learned that certain actions of the body can mean different things. However, there are some actions that are usually interpretated in the same way by everyone.

What message do you get when someone puts his thumb up in the air? If you are like most people, you "hear" the message "something is good" or "everything's OK." What if a sender points her thumb downward? You probably get the opposite message. You probably "hear" the message "something is bad."

There are some actions that give most listeners a negative message. A negative message harms communication. It makes the listener stop receiving your message. Communication comes to a halt.

On the next page is a list of body actions that send negative messages. Read this list. Try to avoid these actions. They will stop you from reaching your communication goal.

# Negative Body Language

| When You: | Receivers "Hear": |
|---|---|
| Look away from the person you're talking to | "I'm not interested in you" "I'd rather talk to someone else." |
| Yawn | "You're boring." "I'm tired." |
| Point at the person you're talking to | "You'd better listen to me or else." "I mean business." |
| Stare at the person you're talking to | "I don't believe you." "I don't believe you." |
| Cross your arms in front of your chest | "I dare you to try anything." "I'm angry with you." |
| Raise your eyebrows at the person you're talking to | "I don't believe you." "You're crazy." |
| Shake a fist at the person you're talking to | "I'm very angry with you." "You're in trouble." |
| Put your hands on your hips as you talk to someone | "I dare you." "I don't believe anything you say." |

## Think About It

Can you add any examples of negative body language to this list? Write the action and its negative meaning in the space provided.

# Positive Body Language

Some types of body language give a positive message to most people. The chart below lists some of these actions. Try to remember the actions on this list. They will help you get your message across to your listener.

| When You: | Listeners "Hear": |
| --- | --- |
| Smile | "I want to be friends." "I like you." |
| Sit up straight | "I'm paying attention." "I'm confident.""I'm proud of myself." |
| Look directly at the person you're talking to | "I want to communicate with you." "I value you." "What I'm saying is important." |
| Walk with your head held high | "I'm a special person." "I believe in myself and my abilities." |
| Nod your head as you talk | "I know what I am talking about.""I agree with you." |
| Touch the person you're talking to lightly on the arm | "You mean a lot to me." "I care about you." |

## Think About It

Can you add any examples of positive body language to this list? Write the action and its positive meaning in the space provided.

## Check What You've Learned

Read each statement. If the statement is true, write T on the answer blank. If the statement is false, write F on the answer blank. (Check your answers on page 120.)

_____ **1.** Most people "hear" a negative message from a frown.

_____ **2.** Avoiding negative body language can help you become a good communicator.

_____ **3.** Using positive body language can help you get your message across to listeners.

# Unit 3 Review

## In this unit:

- You learned that body language is using your body to send messages to others. Body language is powerful. Listeners often "hear" body language messages more than word messages.

- You discovered that certain body action can have different meanings. Good communicators think about the possible messages their actions might send. They match their words with their body language.

- You learned that some actions of the body are interpreted in the same way by many people. Negative body language harms communication. Positive body language helps communication.

## Key Word

(Check your answer on page 120.)

What is body language?

## Key Ideas

Write the answer to each question in the space provided. (Check your answers on page 120.)

1. Why does a good communicator think about body language?

2. Why should your body language match your word message?

**3.** What are four examples of positive body language?

**4.** What are four examples of negative body language?

**5.** Can you be sure of how a listener will interpret your body language? Explain.

**6.** How can you use body language to reach your communication goal?

# What About You? _____

Read about each situation. Think about what you would do. Describe the actions you would take in the space provided.

**1.** Suppose you were meeting someone for the first time. What kind of body language would you use to show the person that you want to know him or her better?

**2.** Suppose you were going for a job interview. What kind of body language would you use to show the person interviewing you that you should get the job?

# It's How You Say It

## In this unit you will:

- discover that carefully choosing your words can help you reach your communication goal.

- identify words that harm communication.

- identify words that help communication.

## Key Words

**conversation:** a spoken exchange of ideas
**express oneself:** to state one's thoughts or feelings

# Meet Tina Parks and Jill Bochenek

Tina Parks and Jill Bochenek are friends. Every Saturday night, they go out. One night they decided to go to a movie. Tina got a newspaper. She checked to see what was playing.

"I've got it," Tina said. "A new horror movie is playing at the Roxy. I love horror movies. That's where we will go."

Jill looked at her. She hated horror movies. They gave her chills. Jill really didn't want to spend her night doing something she disliked.

"Let me see the paper," Jill said. Tina handed it to her. Jill looked over the listings. "Look," she said. "Movies Ten is showing a comedy. My brother saw it last week. He said it was very funny. That's what we should see."

Tina laughed. "How could anybody like that movie? It's about a man who has a baby! That's the stupidest thing I've ever heard of!" Tina then pointed at Jill, and said, "I wouldn't be caught dead seeing that movie!"

Jill frowned. "Well, I think horror movies are stupid," she said. "Who wants to see ugly things? There's enough of that in my real life. When I go out, I want to have a good time. "

"You're such a pain!" Tina yelled. "We always have to do what you want. You never care about anyone but yourself!"

Jill was angry. She jumped up from her chair. "You've got to be kidding! You don't care that I hate horror movies. All you care about is yourself!"

With that, Jill walked toward the door. "I'm going to see the comedy by myself," she said. Then she walked out the door, slamming it shut.

## Think About It

What are the women arguing about? (Check your answer on page 120.)

# LESSON 10

## Unhealthy Communication

Tina Parks and Jill Bochenek are not communicating in a healthy way. Their **conversation**, or spoken exchange of ideas, turned into an argument. Their friendship is in danger.

What caused the argument? It began when the women talked about what movie they should see. Tina wanted to see a horror movie. Jill wanted to see a comedy. The women had different opinions.

It is very normal for two people to feel differently. Every person is different. Every person likes certain things. Every person dislikes certain things. That's OK.

Healthy communication helps people reach an agreement. How? Each person sends a clear message. The message explains the person's feelings. The message may even explain why the person feels that way.

In healthy communication, the message is received by a listener. The listener interprets the message. This information can be used to solve the problem. It gives the listener some idea of how to work things out.

Unhealthy communication stops people from reaching an agreement. Unhealthy communication makes problems worse, not better.

That's what happened to Tina and Jill. Their unhealthy communication made their problem grow into an argument.

What made their communication unhealthy? Both women had negative communication styles. In Unit 2 you learned that a communication style is what you do to get your message across to others. A positive communication style helps a listener receive your message. A negative communication style makes a listener stop hearing your message.

# Tone of Voice

You have learned that the sound of your voice is its tone. A certain tone of voice can help a listener hear your message. Other tones cause the listener to stop hearing the message.

Both Tina and Jill used a negative tone of voice. The women yelled at each other. This made them stop listening. They did not receive a message. They got angry.

Tina laughed when Jill suggested that they see a comedy. The laugh sent Jill a message. It told her that Tina thought her idea was ridiculous. Jill did not feel valued. She did not feel respected. She did not want to be with Tina. So, she went to the movies by herself.

## Think About It

What tone of voice should each woman have used to get her message across? (Check your answer on page 120.)

# Body Language

In Unit 3 you learned that body language is part of your communication style. You discovered that certain actions can help get your message across. Other actions harm communication.

Both Tina and Jill used negative body language. Tina pointed at Jill and said, "I wouldn't be caught dead seeing that movie!" Her body language sent Jill a message. It said, "You'd better do what I say." Jill heard this message. It made her angry.

Jill also used negative body language. At one point, Jill jumped up from her chair. This sudden action sent a message to Tina. It said, "I'm very angry." Jill sent another message when she slammed the door shut. Tina heard, "I'm done with you." These messages stopped their communication.

Think about a time when *you* slammed a door shut. Why did you do this? What message were you trying to send to someone?

# Word Meaning

Tina and Jill used a negative tone of voice and negative body language. There is something else they did to harm communication. They used negative words.

The English language is made up of thousands of words. Some words have very different meanings. *Happy* and *sad* are examples of words that mean totally different things.

Some words have the same basic meaning. *Happy* and *thrilled* are examples of such words. Both *happy* and *thrilled* mean that a person is pleased. But the words show a different degree, or amount, of pleasure. You might be happy to spend a day by yourself. But you'd probably be thrilled to win a lottery!

Describe the last time that you were thrilled.

## Check What You've Learned

Each group of words below has the same basic meaning. However, the words show different degrees or amounts. Think about each word in the group. Underline the word that shows the greatest degree. The first one is done for you. (Check your answers on page 120.)

1. happy        glad        <u>thrilled</u>
2. exhausted        tired        sleepy
3. big        gigantic        large
4. mad        angry        furious
5. unhappy        miserable        sad

# The Power of Words

Communication begins when a speaker sends a message. But the speaker must do two things before he or she says anything. The speaker must decide what the message will be. Then the speaker must decide how to state the message.

Good communicators think about the words they will say. They use words to **express** themselves, or state their thoughts or feelings. They choose words that send a clear message. They choose words that help keep the listener focused. Careful word selection helps speakers reach their communication goals. Good communicators help the listener understand the message.

# Communication Style

Your word selection is part of your communication style. The words you use to get your message across can help you reach your communication goal. Your words can keep communication open. How? Your words can show that you respect your listener. They can make the listener feel valuable. They can tell the listener that you care.

## Check What You've Learned

Read each statement. If the statement is true, write T on the answer blank. If the statement is false, write F on the answer blank. (Check your answers on page 120.)

_____ **1.** A negative communication style can harm communication.

_____ **2.** Some words can harm communication.

_____ **3.** Good communicators don't think about the words they will use to get their message across.

_____ **4.** Good communicators say whatever pops into their heads.

_____ **5.** Carefully choosing your words can help you reach your communication goal.

## Words That Harm Communication

Some words hurt communication. They cause a listener to stop hearing your message. These words create problems rather than solving them. A good communicator is careful to avoid such negative words.

## Words That Blame

Some words show that you hold the listener responsible for something. These words blame the other person. They make the listener feel guilty. They make the listener feel bad. These words cause the listener to stop receiving your message.

Examples of words that show blame are:
- "This is all your fault!"
- "*I* wouldn't have let this happen."
- "How could you have done this?"
- "This would never have happened if you were doing your job!"
- "You really messed this up!"

### What About You?

Suppose you were cooking dinner with a friend. The food took longer to cook than you thought it would take. Your friend said, "Why didn't you start cooking sooner?" Describe how these words would make you feel.

# Words That Show Disrespect

When you call a person a name, you send a negative message. The person hears the message "You are not valuable." The person hears "I don't have respect for you." Name-calling makes a listener feel unworthy. This causes the person to stop listening. Communication stops.

Examples of words that show disrespect are:

- "You idiot! Why did you do that?"
- "I can't believe how stupid you are!"

## What About You?

Think about the last time someone called you a name. Answer these questions about that communication. Write your answers in the space provided.

**1.** What did the speaker say to you?

**2.** How did the words make you feel?

**3.** What effect did it have on your communication?

# Words That Criticize

Some words show that you disapprove of another person. They say that the person is not good at something. Words that criticize make the listener feel bad. They harm communication. Examples of words that criticize are:

- "You really stink at this."
- "How did you ever get this job? You're terrible."
- "What's taking you so long?"
- "I'd be done by now if it wasn't for you."
- "A normal person wouldn't say that."

Suppose you just bought a new shirt. You show a friend what you bought. Your friend says, "Why did you buy that color shirt? You know that color looks terrible on you!" Describe how these words would make you feel.

# Positive Criticism

At times, people will ask you how you feel about something. It is important that you express yourself honestly. This means that sometimes you will have to tell the person you don't like something. Choosing your words carefully will help get your criticism across in a positive manner. For example, you can criticize a child's essay:

**Negative:** This essay is terrible. No wonder you got a D!

**Positive:** You got a D this time, but I know you will do better next time.

## Check What You've Learned

Each pair of statements shows that the speaker dislikes something. One statement sends the message in a positive way. Put a check mark on the answer blank next to each positive statement. (Check your answers on page 120.)

1. _____ "That new hairstyle is very fashionable. But, I'm not sure that it shows off the curl in your hair."

   _____ "What did you do with your hair? You look terrible!"

2. _____ "Why would you possibly want to move there? You won't fit in with anyone."

   _____ "Are you sure that you want to move there? Did you think about how you'll feel in that neighborhood?"

3. _____ "What's wrong with you now?"

_____ "Is everything all right?"

4. _____ "You really stink at this, don't you?"

_____ "I know this is hard to learn. It took me awhile to get the hang of it."

5. _____ "I'm not sure I understand what you mean."

_____ "What are you talking about? You don't make any sense!"

6. _____ "Only a fool would wear an outfit like that!"

_____ "I'm not sure that outfit shows off your figure."

## Always and Never

A good communicator avoids using the words always and never. These words are harsh. They send the message that something is fixed. These words make the listener feel as if the situation is hopeless. It seems as though the situation cannot be changed. Examples of negative communication using these words are:

- "You *always* have to choose what program we watch."
- "I *never* get to use the car."
- "You *never* listen to me."
- "You are *always* in a bad mood."

## What About You?

Think about the last time someone criticized you using the words *always* or *never*. Answer these questions about that communication. Write your answers in the space provided.

1. What did the speaker say to you?

2. How did it make you feel?

3. What effect did the words *always* or *never* have on your communication?

## Think About It

Read each statement. Put a check mark on the answer blank next to the statements that contain words that harm communication. (Check your answers on page 120.)

_____ 1. "I didn't think you were dumb enough to believe that!"

_____ 2. "Do you think that movie would be interesting to you?"

_____ 3. "Perhaps you need to concentrate a little better."

_____ 4. "This is all your fault."

_____ 5. "I should have known better than to ask you to do this."

_____ 6. "I don't understand why you feel that way."

_____ 7. "How did you ever get this job? You don't understand a thing!"

_____ 8. "You never let me go out with my friends."

_____ 9. "You seem a little sad today. Do you want to talk about anything?"

_____ 10. "Stop acting like a jerk! You're embarrassing me."

_____ 11. "That is the stupidest thing I've ever heard!"

## Check What You've Learned

Read each statement. If the statement is true, write T on the answer blank. If the statement is false, write F on the answer blank. (Check your answers on page 120.)

_____ 1. A good communicator avoids using the words _always_ and _never_.

_____ 2. Words that criticize send the message that you like what the listener is doing.

_____ 3. When you give your opinion to someone, it is better to lie than to hurt the person's feelings.

_____ 4. When you call a person a name, you send a negative message.

_____ 5. Some kinds of words can harm communication.

# LESSON 12

## Words That Help Communication

In the last lesson, you learned about words that harm communication. Now it is time to discover words that help communication. By thinking about what you will say, you can keep communication open. You can help a listener stay focused on your message. This helps the listener receive your message. It helps you reach your communication goal.

The following sections describe words that help communication. Carefully read about these words. Then use the words when communicating with others.

## Use I Instead of You

Try to use the word *I* instead of *you* when sending a message. Messages that contain the word *you* are often full of blame. They make the listener feel bad. *You* messages often stop communication.

Instead, try to send *I* messages. An *I* message explains how you feel. It helps the listener understand how you see the situation. An *I* message keeps communication open and positive.

Listed below are pairs of *You* and *I* messages. Read each pair. Think about the message you would rather hear.

*You* **message:** "You are making me very angry."
*I* **message:** "I feel very angry."

*You* **message:** "You don't share your feelings with me."
*I* **message:** "I wish you would tell me about your feelings."

*You* **message:** "You don't make any sense."
*I* **message:** "I am having trouble understanding you."

*You* message: "You don't care what I think."

*I* message: "I feel as if you don't care about how I think."

*You* message: "You disagree with whatever I say."

*I* message: "I feel as if you often disagree with what I say."

## Check What You've Learned

Read each *You* message listed below. Change the message to an *I* message. Write the *I* message in the space provided. (Check your answers on page 121.)

1. *You* message: "You don't listen to what I say!"


2. *You* message: "You are just worried about yourself!"

# Focus on the Problem, Not the Listener

People are all different. They have different ways of doing things. They have different opinions. They want different things. Their needs are different.

You have to get along with others. This means respecting other people's differences. It means working out your differences to reach an agreement. It means solving problems.

Healthy communication can help you work with others. How? Carefully choosing your words can send a positive message to others. Your words can show that you respect the other person. They can tell others that you want to solve the problem. Your words show that you are willing to work toward finding a solution.

Below is a list of positive statements. Each statement is focused on a problem rather than on the listener. Each statement shows that the speaker wants to try to find a solution.

"I understand how you feel. But I feel differently. Let's try to reach an agreement."

"Why don't we spend some time thinking about how we can work this problem out?"

"I don't want this problem to go on any longer. Why don't we talk about how it can be fixed?"

"I guess I made a mistake. I'm sorry. Let's start over again."

"I understand that we have different opinions. Here's what I would like to see happen."

## What About You?

1. Suppose your friend called you. Your friend asked whether you would drive her to a doctor's appointment tomorrow. You said you would. The next day you forgot about the promise. You didn't pick up your friend. She missed the doctor's appointment. Your friend called you that evening. Now she is very mad at you. You don't want to lose her friendship. What could you say to your friend to show that you want to work the problem out? Describe what you would say in the space provided.

2. Now suppose you were the friend. You heard the statement written in the space above. How would the words make you feel? Write your answer in the space provided.

## Use Often or Sometimes

You have already learned that the words *always* and *never* can harm communication. Instead, you should use the words *often* and *sometimes* when being critical. These words are less harsh. They do not make a listener feel blamed. They will keep communication open. Examples of statements that use the words *often* or *sometimes* are:

- "I *often* feel that you aren't listening to me."
- "*Sometimes*, I think that you don't like me."
- "We *often* have to watch your TV programs."
- "*Sometimes*, it seems as if I'm the only one who thinks about cleaning the apartment."

## Check What You've Learned

The statements below contain the words *never* or *always*. Change each statement. Use the words *often* or *sometimes*. Write the new statement in the space provided. (Check your answers on page 121.)

**1.** "You *never* think about me!"

**2.** "I *always* have to take out the garbage."

**3.** "You *never* help me with the chores."

**4.** "You *always* leave your clothes on the floor."

**5.** "I *always* have to answer the telephone."

## Check What You've Learned

Read each statement. If the statement is true, write T on the answer blank. If the statement is false, write F on the answer blank. (Check your answers on page 121.)

_____ **1.** Using the word *I* instead of *you* can make a listener feel blamed for a problem.

_____ **2.** A good communicator uses words that focus on the problem.

_____ **3.** The words *often* and *sometimes* keep communication open.

# Unit 4 Review

## In this unit:

- You learned that carefully choosing your words can help you reach your communication goal. You discovered that good communicators use words that clearly express their thoughts and feelings.

- You discovered that some words harm communication. Words that blame, show disrespect, and criticize make a listener stop hearing your message.

- You identified words that help communication. Using *I* instead of *you*, choosing words that focus on the problem, and using *sometimes* and *often* keep communication open and positive.

## Key Words

Give the meaning of each word. Write your answer in the space provided. (Check your answers on page 121.)

1. Conversation

2. Express

## Key Ideas

Write the answer to each question in the space provided. (Check your answers on page 121.)

1. Why should you think about the words you will use to send a message to others?

**2.** Give two examples of statements that contain words that show disrespect.

**3.** Why does a good communicator avoid using the words *always* and *never* when criticizing?

**4.** Give two examples of statements that focus on the problem, not the listener.

**5.** How do *I* statements help keep communication open?

## What About You?  _____

How will you use what you learned in Unit 4 in your daily life?

# Real World Connection

## The Phone Call

Teah put the phone down. "Wow," she thought. "That was some conversation!" She had just finished speaking with her sister, Liz. Somehow, their talk had turned into an argument.

Teah thought about the conversation. It had started off well. Then Teah asked Liz whether she had plans for the **upcoming** holiday. Liz said that she didn't have any plans. So Teah asked Liz to spend the holiday with her.

That's when the problem started. Liz had gotten very quiet. Then she started yelling at Teah. "I don't need you to take care of me!" she shouted. "My big sister doesn't have to **rescue** me!"

Teah had been confused. "What are you talking about?" she asked.

"You know exactly what I mean," Liz **replied**. " You're the older sister. You think that means you can **rule** my life! You think you can tell me how I have to spend my holidays!"

"No," said Teah. "You don't understand what I'm saying."

"Of course," Liz yelled. "It's always my fault. I never understand anything. That's because I'm the dumb little sister!"

Teah was shocked. She couldn't believe what was happening. "I don't think you're dumb," said Teah. "I think you're a great person. I care a lot about you. I'd like to spend the holiday with you. That's all I'm saying."

"No, it's not," said Liz. "Maybe those are the words you are saying. But you are sending a **quite** different message. You're telling me that I'm not **popular**. You knew that I didn't have any plans for the holiday. Who would want to spend a day with me?"

"That's not true," Teah said. "You have a lot of friends. I didn't know whether you had any plans. That's why I called you. I wanted to find out what you **intended** to do. I thought that, if you were **available**, we could get together. That's all I meant."

Liz was silent. Teah waited a minute. Then she said, "Liz, did you hear me?"

In a low voice, Liz said "Yes, I heard you. What you just said made me feel better. Now I understand why you called." Liz paused for a moment. "I guess I'm a little **irritable** today," she continued. "You see, I had plans to go out tonight. I was really looking forward to it. But the person I was supposed to see just called. He said something had come up. He won't be able to keep our date."

"Oh," said Teah. "Now I understand. You're upset about the canceled plans. I know how you feel. The same thing has happened to me. But you know what I do? I make sure to go out just the same. Even if I have to go alone, I still try to do something special."

"What can I do tonight?" asked Liz.

"Go to the movies with me," Teah replied. "I don't have any plans. I'd love to see the new movie at Cinema Ten.Liz thought for a moment. "I've wanted to see that movie also. What if we go to the 8:00 show?"

"It's a date," Teah answered. "I'll meet you at the movies. Afterward, we can get something to eat. We can talk about our holiday plans then."

The women then hung up. Teah felt good about herself. A problem had **developed** during the conversation. But Teah had worked hard to keep the communication positive. She had carefully selected her words. She tried to stay focused on the problem.  She had kept control of her emotions.

# Key Words_____

In the story, 10 words are in **bold print**. These words
are listed below. Circle the correct meaning for each word.
If you have trouble, go back and read the sentence
containing the word. Look for clues in the sentence. Use
the clues to figure out the meaning of the words. (Check
your answers on page 121.)

1. **Upcoming** means
   a. past.
   b. approaching.
   c. earlier.
   d. growing.

2. **Rescue** means
   a. wait.
   b. harm.
   c. fix.
   d. save.

3. **Replied** means
   a. yelled.
   b. asked.
   c. answered.
   d. cried.

4. **Rule** means
   a. overcome.
   b. measure.
   c. destroy.
   d. control.

5. **Quite** means
   a. low.
   b. very.
   c. few.
   d. soft.

6. **Popular** means
   a. hated.
   b. funny.
   c. well liked.
   d. lovable.

7. **Intended** means
   a. planned.
   b. caused.
   c. disliked.
   d. allowed.

8. **Available** means
   a. busy.
   b. free.
   c. happy.
   d. eager.

9. **Irritable** means
   a. pleased.
   b. injured.
   c. cranky.
   d. thrilled.

10. **Developed** means
    a. begun.
    b. ended.
    c. lessened.
    d. improved.

# Check What You've Learned

Circle the letter of the best answer to each question.

(Check your answers on page 121.)

1. Teah and Liz are
   a. parents.
   b. cousins.
   c. sisters.
   d. neighbors.

2. Teah had called Liz to find out whether she
   a. wanted to see a movie.
   b. could baby-sit.
   c. was in a good mood.
   d. had holiday plans.

3. Liz got angry because she thought Teah was trying to
   a. rule her life.
   b. ignore her.
   c. cancel their plans.
   d. make fun of her.

4. What word describes how Teah's words make Liz feel?
   a. Tired
   b. Proud
   c. Happy
   d. Dumb

5. What message does Liz hear from Teah?
   a. She is pretty.
   b. She is smart.
   c. She is not popular.
   d. She is interesting.

6. Why is Liz irritable?
   a. She worked a double shift.
   b. Her date was canceled.
   c. She doesn't like Teah.
   d. She is exhausted.

7. What does Teah do whenever she has a canceled date?
   a. She still goes out.
   b. She calls Liz
   c. She stays home and cries.
   d. She reads a book.

8. What did the women decide to do?
   a. Go shopping.
   b. Go see a movie.
   c. Stop talking to each other.
   d. Take a walk together.

9. How did Teah feel about herself after the conversation?
   a. Unhappy
   b. Good
   c. Worried
   d. Confused

10. What did good communication skills help Teah do?
    a. Make plans for the holiday
    b. Argue with Liz
    c. Work out a problem
    d. See a movie

# UNIT 5

# Listen Carefully

## In this unit you will:

- discover how listening helps communication.
- develop a good listening attitude.
- explore ways to show a person that you are listening.

## Key Words

**attitude:** a person's way of acting, thinking, or feeling
**assume:** to take something for granted

# Meet Al Ramirez and Chico Torres

Al and Chico share an apartment. They have one TV set. Al had bought it before he moved in with Chico. That worked out well because Chico did not have a TV.

Most nights, Chico gets home before Al does. He usually turns on the TV. He likes to watch sports programs.

One night, Al came home late. He was very tired. It had been a very long day.

As Al walked toward the apartment, he looked at his watch. "Good," he thought. "My favorite show will be starting in five minutes. I'll just get home in time to watch it."

Then Al thought of Chico. Al frowned. "He does nothing but watch sports," Al thought. "He's probably watching a game right now."

Al felt himself getting angry. What would he do if Chico was already watching something? It would probably be something that Al didn't like.

Al opened the door to the apartment. Sure enough, Chico was in front of the TV. He was watching a football game. The score was tied. Chico watched closely. He didn't even notice Al.

Al walked right over to the set. He changed the channel.

"Hey," yelled Chico. "What do you think you're doing?" he asked.

Al did not reply. He just sat down in a chair.

"Did you hear me?" shouted Chico. "I asked you what you think you're doing."

"I'm watching a show," said Al. "I'm tired of always watching whatever you want," he said to his friend.

Chico looked at Al. "This is an important game," he said. "My favorite team is playing. They need to win in order to reach the championships."

"I don't really care about your football team," replied Al. "My favorite show is on. That's what I am going to watch."

Chico paused for a minute. He thought about what he wanted to tell Al. He thought about the words he should use. Then he said, "Al, you're not listening to me. I'm trying to tell you that this is a very special game. It is important to me that I watch it."

"I watch a certain show every week. It's on right now. I want to watch it. I don't want to talk about football anymore," said Al.

Chico got very angry. He felt as if he was going to burst.

"You never care about anything but yourself," shouted Chico. "It always has to be your way."

"Who's TV is it anyway?" Al asked. "Mine. Therefore, I get to choose the program."

Chico was furious. "That stupid TV is the only thing you own in this whole place. Everything else belongs to me! But I still let you use things."

Al looked at his friend. "OK," he said. "From now on, I'll use only the things that belong to me. You use only the things that belong to you."

Chico smiled. "Fine. I can do that," he said. Then he added, "By the way, get out of my chair!"

## Think About It

Write the answer to each question in the space provided. (Check your answers on page 121.)

1. What are the men arguing about?


2. Why does Chico want to watch the football game?


3. Why does Al want to watch his show?

## Listening and Communication

You have learned that three things are needed for communication to happen. First, there must be a sender. The sender is the person who starts the communication. Second, there must be a message. The message is the idea the sender wants to share. Third, there must be a receiver. The receiver gets the message from the sender. If any of the three parts is missing, communication does not happen.

### What About You?

How do you feel when someone doesn't listen to what you are saying? Describe your feelings in the space provided.

## Communication Breakdown

You just read about a conversation between Al Ramirez and Chico Torres. Did communication happen? No. That is because only two parts of communication were present. There was a sender. There was a message. What was missing? Neither man listened to the other. Without a listener, communication ended.

Al and Chico heard each other's words. But neither man actually listened to the message. They talked *at* each other, not *with* each other. This caused their communication to break down.

The breakdown led to other problems. The men got angry with one another. Their emotions got in the way of their communication. They did not choose their words carefully. They said things they would not normally say.

Good communication skills would have helped Al and Chico solve their disagreement. Positive communication would have helped the men work things out.

## What About You?

This activity will help you rate your ability to listen. Read each statement. Circle the number that best describes you.

**1.** When people talk to me, I listen to what they have to say.

| 5 | 4 | 3 | 2 | 1 |
|---|---|---|---|---|
| Always | | Sometimes | | Never |

**2.** I make sure a speaker knows that I am listening.

| 5 | 4 | 3 | 2 | 1 |
|---|---|---|---|---|
| Always | | Sometimes | | Never |

**3.** I listen to people who disagree with me.

| 5 | 4 | 3 | 2 | 1 |
|---|---|---|---|---|
| Always | | Sometimes | | Never |

**4.** If someone tells me something I don't like, I still keep listening.

| 5 | 4 | 3 | 2 | 1 |
|---|---|---|---|---|
| Always | | Sometimes | | Never |

**5.** I listen as much as I talk.

| 5 | 4 | 3 | 2 | 1 |
|---|---|---|---|---|
| Always | | Sometimes | | Never |

**6.** Even if I don't understand what someone is saying, I keep on listening.

| 5 | 4 | 3 | 2 | 1 |
|---|---|---|---|---|
| Always | | Sometimes | | Never |

**7.** When someone is speaking to me, I do not interrupt.

| 5 | 4 | 3 | 2 | 1 |
|---|---|---|---|---|
| Always | | Sometimes | | Never |

Look at the numbers you circled. Did you circle the number 3 or a lower number for any of the statements? If so, this is an area that probably needs a little work.

## Think About It

Think about the last time you argued with someone. Then answer these questions about that negative communication.

**1.** What message did you try to send to the other person?

**2.** Do you think that the other person listened to your message? Why do you feel this way?

**3.** Did you listen to the other person's message? Explain why.

**4.** How could good listening skills have helped you solve the problem?

## Check What You've Learned

Read each statement. If the statement is true, write T on the answer blank. If the statement is false, write F on the answer blank. (Check your answers on page 121.)

_____ **1.** A good communicator is also a good listener.

_____ **2.** Spoken communication can happen without a listener.

_____ **3.** Good listening skills can help solve problems with others.

# LESSON 14

## Develop a Good Listening Attitude

Listening is part of communicating. In order to be a good communicator, you have to be a good listener. Being a good listener starts before a speaker even says a word. It starts with the way you approach the communication. It starts with your attitude.

Your **attitude** is the way you act, think, or feel about something. Your attitude affects your thoughts and actions. It determines how you approach a communication. A positive attitude helps the sending and receiving of messages. A negative attitude stops the passing of messages between people.

Remember Al Ramirez and Chico Torres? Their communication was negative. It turned into an argument. There were many reasons this happened. One reason was Al's attitude. On his way to the apartment, he thought about Chico. He thought about how Chico always watched sports. This made Al angry. It made Al feel as if Chico cared only about himself. It made Al feel as if he didn't count.

Al went into the apartment with a negative attitude. He **assumed**, or took for granted, that Chico would be watching a sports program. Sure enough, that's what he discovered. This made Al even madder. He reacted strongly.

Al's attitude interfered with their communication. Al assumed that he knew why Chico wanted to watch the football game. He figured that Chico thought he could do whatever he wanted. Al didn't bother to listen to Chico's explanation. He didn't hear that this game was very important to Chico. Because neither Al nor Chico was listening, their communication stopped.

# Be Positive

What if Al had gone into the apartment with a different attitude? Suppose he had thought, "I really want to watch my favorite show. If Chico already has a game on, I'll ask him if he really has to watch it. Then I'll tell him why my show is important to me. Maybe we can come to an agreement."

## Think About It

What do you think would have happened if Al had gone into the apartment with this attitude? (Check your answers on page 121.)

# Keep Communication Open

A positive attitude keeps communication open. It helps a listener hear the message sent by the sender. A positive attitude also helps the listener interpret the message. Good communicators approach a conversation with a positive attitude.

## Check What You've Learned

Read the statements below. If a statement shows a positive attitude, put a + on the answer blank. If the statement shows a negative attitude, put a – on the answer blank. (Check your answers on page 121.)

_____ 1. "She's not going to listen to one word I say."

_____ 2. "I'm going to try my best to work things out with him."

_____ 3. "Whatever he says, I will keep my emotions under control."

_____ 4. "I'm really going to try to understand how she feels about this."

**77**

_____ 5. "I don't know why I'm even bothering to talk to him."

_____ 6. "She won't understand what I mean."

_____ 7. "I really want to get his opinion on this."

_____ 8. "He is so stubborn! He'll never change his mind."

_____ 9. "This is going to be a total waste of my time."

_____ 10. "I know that if I use the right words, I can make her understand how I feel."

_____ 11. "If he starts getting angry, I'm just going to walk away."

_____ 12. "She's so stupid. She'll never understand me!"

_____ 13. "I don't know why I'm trying to talk to her. All she cares about is herself."

_____ 14. "I know that we can work out our differences."

_____ 15. "I will not get angry, no matter what he says."

## How to Develop a Good Listening Attitude

A good listening attitude can help you in your everyday life. How? A good listening attitude can help you work out problems with others. It can help you communicate in a positive way.

Listed below are some things that you can do to develop a good listening attitude.

## 1. Treat Others With Respect

Your attitude shows how you feel about the person you are communicating with. A positive attitude shows that you respect the other person. It shows that you value the person. It shows that you honor his or her thoughts and feelings.

Does this mean that you have to agree with the other person? No. You have your own thoughts and feelings. They can be different from those of other people. That's OK. That's your right.

You want others to value your opinion. In the same way, other people want you to value their opinions. Your actions show this respect.

## 2. Be Willing to Change Your Communication Goal

You have learned that you communicate to reach a certain goal. Your goal is the reason you are involved in the communication.

Sometimes, you will have to change your goal in the middle of a conversation. Why? You need to do this when you have learned new information. The new information changes the focus of the conversation. It changes your goal.

Suppose you have started a conversation with a friend. Your friend has let you down. He was supposed to give you a ride somewhere. But your friend never showed up. You are disappointed with your friend. Your communication goal is to share your feelings with your friend.

However, as you begin the communication, your friend tells you that he had an accident on the way to your home. This is information you didn't have. Your feelings change. Your communication goal changes. You want to know about your friend's feelings. You want to know whether he is OK. The focus of the conversation changes from your feelings to his.

## 3. Don't Make Assumptions

Try not to make assumptions when you communicate. Don't believe that you know exactly how the person will behave. Don't think that you know exactly how the person feels. Doing so can cause you to miss important information. It will stop you from hearing the person's message.

Instead, try to keep an open mind. Don't think about past communications with the person. Start fresh. This will keep the communication positive.

### 4. Keep Your Emotions Under Control

Emotions are strong feelings. They can make you stop listening. They interrupt communication.

If you feel emotions coming out, stop the conversation. Take a minute to calm yourself down. Say to the other person, "I need a minute to myself." Then walk away. Don't continue the communication until you are in control. Then try again.

## Think About It

In each communication described below, someone makes a mistake. Think about what the person could have done to show a good listening attitude. Name the mistake. Then explain what the person could have done to keep the communication open. (Check your answers on page 121.)

1. Miko heard Tao call his name. "Oh, great," Miko thought. "Every time I talk with Tao we wind up having an argument. He thinks he knows everything." In an angry voice, Miko said, "What do you want?"

   Mistake:

   Suggestion:

2. Ryan walked up to Chuck. He began telling Chuck about his date the night before. Chuck listened for a minute. Then he turned his back on Ryan and walked away.

   Mistake:

   Suggestion:

**3.** Rhea and Tom are talking about their relationship. Tom says that he wants to date other people. Rhea starts to cry. This makes Tom feel uncomfortable.

Mistake:


Suggestion:


**4.** Alex feels that Joan spends too much time with her friends. He wants to let Joan know that he feels as if she doesn't care about him. Alex tells Joan he needs to talk to her. He says, "You've been spending a lot of time with your girlfriends lately. We haven't had much time together." Joan replies, "I know. One of my friends has a health problem. We've been getting together to try and help her out." Alex continues, "I feel as if you don't care about me anymore."

Mistake:


Suggestion:


## Check What You've Learned

Read each statement. If the statement is true, write T on the answer blank. If the statement is false, write F on the answer blank. (Check your answers on page 121.)

_____ **1.** A good listening attitude can help you interpret a speaker's message.

_____ **2.** Thinking about past communications with a speaker helps you understand the message sent in a new communication.

_____ **3.** Showing strong emotions can help you send a message to another person.

_____ **4.** You should always stick to your original communication goal.

_____ **5.** People with good listening attitudes show respect for others.

# LESSON 15

## Show That You Are Listening

It is important to show a speaker that you are listening. One way to do this is by using positive body language. Nod your head as the person talks. Sit up straight. Make eye contact. All these acts send a message to the speaker. They say, "I am paying attention to you. I am listening to your words. I want to understand your message."

You can also use certain words to show that you are listening. As the speaker pauses, say, "Tell me more" or "That's interesting." These phrases send a message. They tell the speaker that you respect his or her words and feelings. These words show that you are listening carefully. They show that you are interested.

## Check What You've Learned

Read each statement below. If the words show that you are listening, put a check mark on the answer blank. (Check your answers on page 121.)

___ 1. "You really know a lot about this. Tell me more."

___ 2. "You aren't making any sense."

___ 3. "I don't understand what you want."

___ 4. "I don't agree. But I do see why you feel that way."

___ 5. "I'd really like to hear your opinion of this."

___ 6. "You've got everything all wrong."

___ 7. "Could you explain that to me again?"

___ 8. "You are really helping me understand this."

___ 9. "I have no idea what you are talking about."

___ 10. "Please go on. I am very interested in what you have to say."

# Show That You Understand

A listener has to do more than simply hear a speaker's words. A listener must also interpret a message. This means identifying a speaker's ideas. It means understanding a speaker's feelings.

You can show that you understand a speaker's message by repeating his or her words. In the following conversation, Bill does this.

DONNA: I can't go out with you tonight.

BILL: Why not?

DONNA: I promised Tracey I'd watch her baby. If you make a promise, you have to keep it.

BILL: That's right. If you make a promise, you have to keep to it.

Another way to show that you understand a speaker's ideas or feelings is to restate the message in your own words. In the following conversation, Tony does this.

ALEX: I'd never vote for that person.

TONY: Why not?

ALEX: He makes all kinds of promises but never does what he said he would.

TONY: So, you think that a mayor should do what he promises?

ALEX: That's right.

## Think About It

Read each statement. Think about how you would respond. Carefully choose words that show you understand the speaker's message. Write your response in the space provided.

1. "Every time I am 10 minutes late, you think I am hiding something from you."
   Response:

**2.** "I don't like you hanging out with that guy. He's going to get you in trouble someday."

Response: _____

**3.** "I don't want to go to that club anymore. Every time you're there, you end up drinking too much."

Response: _____

## Check What You've Learned

Read each statement. If the statement is true, write T on the answer blank. If the statement is false, write F on the answer blank. (Check your answers on page 121.)

____ **1.** Positive body language can show a speaker that you are listening.

____ **2.** A listener must interpret messages.

____ **3.** The only way to show that you understand a speaker is by repeating his or her exact words.

# Unit 5 Review

## In this unit:

- You learned that listening is an important part of communication. Without listening, communication stops.

- You discovered that a good listening attitude helps keep communication open. People with good listening attitudes treat others with respect, are willing to change their communication goals, don't make assumptions, and keep their emotions under control.

- You learned that positive body language and carefully chosen words tell a speaker that you are listening. Repeating the speaker's words, exactly or in your own words, shows that you understand the speaker's thoughts and feelings.

## Key Words

Explain the meaning of each word. Write your answer in the space provided. (Check your answers on page 121.)

1. Attitude

2. Assume

## Key Ideas

Write the answer to each question in the space provided. (Check your answers on page 121.)

1. Can communication happen without listening? Explain.

**2.** What is a good listening attitude?

**3.** What are four things you can do to develop a good listening attitude?

**4.** How does making an assumption stop communication?

**5.** Why does changing your communication goal show a speaker that you are listening?

**6.** Describe two kinds of body language that show a speaker that you are listening.

**7.** Explain how you can show a speaker that you understand his or her thoughts and feelings.

**8.** Explain how listening carefully can help you solve problems with others.

## What About You? _____

Think about what you have learned in this unit. Then answer these questions. Write your answer in the space provided.

**1.** Name three things that you learned in this unit.

**2.** How will you use this information in your everyday life?

# Put Yourself In Their Shoes

## In this unit you will:

- understand the meaning of point of view.
- look at events from different points of view.
- discover that understanding another person's point of view helps resolve conflict.

## Key Words

**point of view:** the way a person thinks about people or events
**conflict:** disagreement

# Meet Yolanda Turner

Yolanda Turner has a little girl only five months old. Yolanda isn't working right now. She can't afford child care for the baby. So Yolanda stays home.

Once in a while, Yolanda makes a little money baby-sitting. But her baby-sitting jobs are few.

Yolanda doesn't have much money. She can't remember the last time she bought new clothes. She doesn't even have a telephone because it would cost too much.

Yolanda does get some support checks. But they usually don't cover all her bills. Since the baby was born, Yolanda's food bills have increased. She needs formula for the baby. She needs diapers. All these things cost money— money that Yolanda doesn't have.

In Yolanda's neighborhood is a small market. The owner, Mrs. Booth, is a kind person. She and Yolanda have an arrangement. Mrs. Booth lets Yolanda buys things on credit. She keeps a record of the money Yolanda owes her.

Yolanda has agreed to give Mrs. Booth at least $10 every week. It is all she can afford. Even with this weekly payment, Yolanda's bill is adding up.

One day, Yolanda went to the market to get diapers for the baby. Mrs. Booth saw her. She asked Yolanda to go to the back of the store.

"Yolanda," Mrs. Booth began, "I need to talk to you about something. I was looking at my books last night. I was surprised to find how much money you owe me."

Yolanda blushed. "I know it's adding up," she said. "But the baby was sick last week. I needed some extra things. I needed aspirin and a thermometer. They made the bill a bit higher than normal."

"You also forgot to give me $10 last week," Mrs. Booth said gently.

"I had to give it to the electric company. They were

threatening to shut off my electricity," Yolanda replied.

"I'm sorry to hear the baby was sick," Mrs. Booth said. "But I'm afraid that I can't let you sign for anything else. If you want something, you'll have to pay cash."

Yolanda grew angry. "What do you mean?" she cried. "You can't just stop our agreement. We have a deal."

A sad look crossed Mrs. Booth's face. "That's right, Yolanda. We did have a deal. You didn't keep your part. Now, I'm afraid that I won't be able to keep my part."

Yolanda didn't speak. She just stood there ready to cry. Mrs. Booth saw how upset she was. "I'm sorry, Yolanda," she said. "I have money problems of my own right now. I just can't let this keep going on."

Yolanda struck her hand on a counter. "You don't understand," she shouted. "I need diapers. I don't have any more left for my baby."

"You can have the diapers," Mrs. Booth replied. "But only if you pay cash for them. I'm sorry. But I can't help you anymore."

Yolanda rushed toward the door. She was embarrassed. She felt as if everyone was against her. Mrs. Booth walked back into the market. She also felt like everyone was against her.

## Think About It

Circle the answer that best completes each sentence. (Check your answers on page 122.)

1. Yolanda needs to get
   a. some formula for the baby.
   b. a new shirt for herself.
   c. diapers for the baby.
   d. a thermometer.

2. Yolanda couldn't give Mrs. Booth $10 last week because she
   a. bought a new car.
   b. gave the money to the electric company.
   c. lost the money.
   d. thought her bill was paid up.

**89**

# LESSON 16

## What Is Point of View?

Right now you are looking at this book. You see it a certain way. Your position determines your view of the book. You might be sitting down and looking directly at the book. You might be standing up and looking down at the book. Each position gives you a slightly different view of the book.

You also have a view of the things that happen in your life. The way you think about these things is determined by your position. This is called your point of view. **Point of view** is the way you think about the events you experience and the people you meet.

You know that every person is different. Every person is unique. No two people have had the same experiences. As a result, different people see things in a slightly different way. People have different points of view.

## Think About It

Does anyone else see life in exactly the same way that you do? Explain why or why not. (Check your answers on page 122.)

# Different Points of View

Think about the conversation between Yolanda Turner and Mrs. Booth. The women have something in common. They made an agreement with each other. The agreement has now fallen apart.

Yolanda looks at the problem from her point of view. She feels that Mrs. Booth is causing the problem. Yolanda thinks that Mrs. Booth is being unfair. Yolanda missed paying her $10 only once. Just because of that one miss, Mrs. Booth wants to stop their arrangement.

Mrs. Booth looks at the same problem from her point of view. Her view of the problem is different from Yolanda's. Mrs. Booth thinks that Yolanda has taken advantage of her. Yolanda has let her bill get very high. She also skipped a payment. Mrs. Booth runs a business. She has her own bills to pay. She can't afford to let people take things from her store without any payment.

# Understanding Another's Point of View

Yolanda and Mrs. Booth have different points of view. Yolanda sees the problem one way. Mrs. Booth sees the problem another way. Neither person is totally right. Neither person is totally wrong. They are just different.

Yolanda and Mrs. Booth need to solve their problem. They need to come to some kind of agreement. Their first step is to try to understand the other person's point of view.

How do you understand another person's point of view? You have to try to put yourself in the other person's shoes. You have to try to look at the event from the other person's position. You have to try to see what the other person sees. You have to forget about yourself for a minute. You have to try to think about the other person.

Understanding another person's point of view takes work. It means listening carefully to what the person says. It means thinking about the person's life.

Is it worth the effort? Definitely. Being able to see things from another person's point of view will help you in your everyday life. This skill will help you get along with others. It will help you solve problems.

Read about the following situations. Name the problem that the people face. Then think about each person's view of the situation. Describe their points of view in the space provided. (Check your answers on page 122.)

1. Ike asks Tim whether he can borrow Tim's car. Ike has met someone special. He wants to ask her out for a date. But Ike doesn't have a car. A few months ago, Ike was in a bad accident. His car was totaled. Tim just got his car. He's very proud of it. Tim takes good care of the car. He treats it as if it were a person. Tim does not like the idea of letting Ike drive the car. Tim thinks Ike is a poor driver. He has seen Ike drive over the speed limit.

**Problem:**


**Ike's point of view:**


**Tim's point of view:**


2. Joe and Kay just started dating. They have been seeing each other for about a month. They get along really well. Kay wants to introduce Joe to her friends. Her friend Tanya is having a big party next week. All her friends will be there. She wants Joe to go to the party with her. Joe doesn't like big parties. They make him feel uncomfortable. He doesn't want to go to Tanya's party. Everyone else will know each other. He will know only Kay. Joe would rather spend the night alone with Kay.

**Problem:**




**Kay's point of view:**




**Joe's point of view:**




3. Mike and Bud are roommates. Mike loves pets. When he was a kid, he had a dog. Mike found a stray dog near the apartment building. He took the dog home with him. Mike takes good care of the dog. He pays for all its food. Mike wants to keep the dog permanently. Bud doesn't like pets. He doesn't want an animal running around the apartment. Bud is worried that the dog will ruin his things. He already found the dog chewing on a pair of his socks. Bud wants Mike to get rid of the dog.

**Problem:**




**Mike's point of view:**




**Bud's point of view:**

## Check What You've Learned

Read each statement. If the statement is true, write T on the answer blank. If the statement is false, write F on the answer blank. (Check your answers on page 122.)

_____ 1. People usually see events the same way.

_____ 2. Understanding another person's point of view means thinking about the other person.

_____ 3. Listening is an important part of understanding another person's point of view.

_____ 4. Understanding another person's point of view can cause problems.

_____ 5. Seeing things from another person's point of view is a skill that you can use in everyday life.

## Solving Conflicts

You deal with other people every day of your life. Each person you meet is different from you. Each person has a different point of view.

The differences among people can sometimes lead to conflicts. A **conflict** is a disagreement. Conflict is a natural part of life. It is a part of change.

In order to get along with others, you need to know how to deal with conflict. You need to know how to solve a disagreement.

Luckily, there is a list of steps you can follow to solve a conflict. Following these steps will help you find solutions to your problems.

### Step 1: Name the Problem

Every conflict has two sides. The two sides do not agree on something. They oppose one another.

The first step in solving a conflict is to name the problem. Be sure that you clearly understand what the two sides disagree about. Name the problem. This gives you a clear picture of what is wrong. It helps to keep you focused on the problem.

### Step 2: See Both Points of View

Each side looks at the problem a certain way. Each side has a different point of view.

In order to work things out, you need to see the problem from each point of view. First think about how you see the situation. Then think about how the other person sees the same situation.

### Step 3: List Possible Solutions

Make a list of ways to solve the problem. Write down everything you think of on the list. Don't throw out any ideas. At this point, every idea is a good idea.

### Step 4: Examine the List

Look over the list of ideas. Think about the first solution. Think about how it would affect one side. Think about how it would affect the other side. Think about what might happen as a result. If you feel that it is a good solution, circle it. Then go on and consider the next idea listed. Evaluate each idea.

### Step 5: Find the Solution

At this point, you will probably have a few ideas circled. Think about which solution will help *both* sides of the problem. Decide upon your final solution.

## Using the Steps

You have just read about a plan for solving conflicts. Now let's see how two people used this plan to solve a problem. Turn back to page 92. Read about the problem between Ike and Tim. Let's see how these individuals used the plan to solve their problem.

### Step 1: Name the Problem.

Ike wants to borrow Tim's car. Tim is uncomfortable about lending the car to Ike.

### Step 2: See Both Points of View.

Ike wants to take out the person he met. He feels that he can take her out only if he can drive.

Tim is very proud of his car. He takes good care of it. Tim doesn't think that Ike would take good care of his car. He feels that Ike is a poor driver. Tim doesn't want Ike to get in an accident with his car. He doesn't want Ike to smash up his car the way he did with his own.

## Step 3: List Possible Solutions.

Here are some ways the men can solve their problem:

1. Tim can lend his car to Ike.

2. Tim can tell Ike that he can't borrow his car.

3. Ike can forget about this kind of date until he has his own car.

4. Tim can drive Ike and his date.

5. Tim can ask someone out that same night. The two couples can go out together.


## Step 4: Examine the List.

Now it's time to look at each item on the list. Think about how each item would affect both Ike and Tim.

1. If Tim lends his car to Ike, Ike will be pleased. He will be able to go on his date. But Tim will not be pleased. He will have loaned his car to someone whom he feels is a poor driver.

2. If Tim refuses to let Ike use his car, Tim won't have to worry about Ike's driving. This will make Tim happy. But Ike will not be able to go on his date. This will make Ike unhappy.

3. If Ike waits until he has a car of his own, he may never date this special person. This will make Ike unhappy. He really wants to spend some time with this woman. This solution will make Tim happy. He won't have to worry about Ike driving his car.

4. If Tim drives Ike, he won't have to worry about his car. He will be the one in charge of it. This will make Tim happy. This solution will still allow Ike to go on his date.

5. If Tim and Ike both have dates the same night, they will both be happy. Tim won't have to worry about his car. Ike will be able to see his special person.

**Step 5: Find the Solution.**

Ike and Tim would probably circle the fourth and fifth ideas on the list. Each of these ideas suits both men. These ideas suit each point of view. Either of these ideas would be a good solution to the problem.

## Agree to Disagree

Ike and Tim used the problem-solving plan. They were able to find a solution to their problem. Each man was happy with the solution.

Not all conflicts can be solved this easily. Sometimes, you won't be able to reach an agreement. In these cases, you will simply have to *agree to disagree*. This means saying, "We just can't work things out." It means that you've tried to find a solution but nothing works.

## Check What You've Learned _____

1. Listed below are the five steps to problem solving. They are not in the correct order. Put them in the proper order. Write the number 1 next to the first step, 2 by the second step, and so on. The last step should be 5. (Check your answers on page 122.)

   _____ Examine the list

   _____ Name the problem

   _____ Find the solution

   _____ List possible solutions

   _____ See both points of view

Read each statement. If the statement is true, write T on the answer blank. If the statement is false, write F on the answer blank.

_____ **2.** Every problem has two different sides.

_____ **3.** A problem can be solved in many different ways.

_____ **4.** A good solution takes into account only one side of the problem.

_____ **5.** Looking at a problem from another person's point of view can help find a solution to the problem.

_____ **6.** Sometimes the only way to solve a problem is to agree to disagree.

# Unit 6 Review

## In this unit:

- You found that people are different. Their differences cause them to see things in different ways. The way a person thinks about another person or an event is called that person's point of view.

- You learned that in order to understand another person's point of view, you need to think about the other person. You need to think about that person's life. You need to try to look at a situation the way that person would. Doing so will give you information about the person and the problem. It will help you think of ways to solve the problem.

- You discovered that conflict is a part of life. You can work out conflicts with others by following a five-step plan. With this plan, you must name the problem, see both points of view, list possible solutions, examine the list, and then find the best solution.

## Key Words

Explain the meaning of each term below. Write your answer in the space provided. (Check your answers on page 122.)

**1.** Point of view

**2.** Conflict

## Key Ideas

(Check your answers on page 122.)

**1.** Why do people have different points of view?

**2.** Name some things you should do when trying to look at a problem from another person's point of view.

**3.** What are five steps you should follow when you are trying to solve a conflict?

**4.** What is a good solution?

**5.** What does the phrase *agree to disagree* mean?

## What About You?

Think about a conflict that you face now. If you do not have any conflicts right now, think about a past conflict. Use the steps in the conflict-solving plan to find a solution to your problem.

**Step 1:**

**Step 2:**

**Step 3:**

**Step 4:**

**Step 5:**

# UNIT 7

# Put It Into Practice

## In this unit you will:

- review the key ideas of this book.
- practice good communication skills.
- show that you know how to be a good communicator.

# Be Proud of Yourself

You have learned a great deal by working through this book. You discovered what it means to communicate in a healthy way. You learned ways to keep communication open and positive. You explored ways of improving your own communication style.

Working through this book taught you many new skills. You can use these communication skills every day of your life. They will help you get your message across to others. They will help you receive others' messages. They will even help you solve conflicts with others.

In this unit, you will practice the skills that you have learned. The practice will help make your skills stronger. The practice will help you become a good communicator.

# Reviewing Unit 1: Getting the Message Across

In Unit 1 you discovered what is needed for communication to happen. You thought about why people communicate. You learned skills that keep communication healthy.

Think about these things. Look back at Unit 1. Then work through the following activities. They will strengthen the skills you developed in Unit 1.

## Think About It

Use your own words to describe communication. Write your answer in the space provided. (Check your answers on page 122.)

You have learned that communication needs a sender, a message, and a receiver. Read each communication below. Name the sender, message, and receiver. Write your answer in the space provided. (Check your answers on page 122.)

**1.** SEAN TO RYAN: I can't go to the store with you today. I have to work.

Sender:

Message:

Receiver:

**2.** PAT TO CARLA: I'm so upset! I had an accident on my way home.

Sender:

Message:

Receiver:

**3.** JIM TO MARK: You're never going to believe what happened! My father just gave me two tickets to tonight's baseball game.

Sender:

Message:

Listener:

**4.** EVA TO ZOE: I didn't sleep at all last night. The baby was sick.

Sender:

Message:

Listener:

## Think About It

(Check your answers on page 122.)

**1.** Use your own words to explain what a communication goal is. Write your explanation in the space provided.

**2.** You have learned that there are six common communication goals. List these goals in the space provided.

**3.** Name four things that you can do to keep communication healthy.

## Check What You've Learned

Read each pair of statements. Underline the statement that shows healthy communication skills. (Check your answers on page 122.)

**1.** "You never make any sense."

"I'm not sure I understand what you mean."

2. "I understand why you feel that way. But I feel differently."

   "Anyone who feels that way is crazy!"

3. "Why would you possibly want to do that?"

   "I would not want to do that."

4. "I don't think you have all the facts straight."

   "You don't know what you're talking about."

5. "You better do what I tell you."

   "I'd appreciate it if you would try to do what I ask."

6. "I would really enjoy hearing how you feel about this."

   "You never tell me how you feel."

7. "That outfit looks silly on you."

   "I'm not sure that outfit suits you."

8. "It would make me happy to choose the movie tonight."

   "You never let me decide what movie to see."

9. "Sometimes I feel as if you don't listen to me."

   "You never listen to what I say."

10. "You always make me late."

    "I'd like to be on time tonight."

## Reviewing Unit 2: A Matter of Style

In Unit 2 you learned about communication styles. You discovered how communication styles affect communication. You found out why people have different communication styles.

Think about these things. Look back at Unit 2. Then work through the following activities. They will strengthen the skills you developed in Unit 2.

## Think About It

(Check your answers on page 123.)

1. Write your answer in the space provided. Use your own words to explain what a communication style is.


2. Name four things that make up your communication style.


3. Do emotions help or hurt communication? Explain.


You learned that good communicators match their tone of voice with their message. Think about each message listed below. Describe the tone of voice you would use to say each message. Be sure that they match.

4. "I love you."


5. "I have a problem."


6. "I enjoy spending time with you."


7. "I am furious about what you did."


8. "I'm sorry."


## Check What You've Learned

You have learned that people have different communication styles. A good communicator keeps this in mind when communicating with others. Read each statement about communication styles. If a statement is true, write T on the answer blank. If a statement is false, write F on the answer blank. (Check your answers on page 123.)

_____ 1. Everyone feels that looking directly at a speaker is a sign of respect.

_____ **2.** Different people need different amounts of personal space.

_____ **3.** Some people feel that it is normal for a person to be late for an appointment.

_____ **4.** No one likes to be embraced by a stranger.

_____ **5.** Some people avoid making eye contact in order to show respect for the speaker.

## What About You?

How do you feel about making eye contact with a speaker? Do you think that looking directly at a speaker is a sign of respect or disrespect? Describe your feelings in the space provided.

# Reviewing Unit 3: You Can't Hear It

In Unit 3 you learned about body language and its effect on communication. You thought about the messages you send with your body. You discovered how you can use body language to help get your message across to others.

Think about these things. Look back at Unit 3. Then work through the following activities. They will strengthen the skills you developed in Unit 3.

## Think About It

Use your own words to explain what body language is. Write your explanation in the space provided. (Check your answers on page 123.)

## Think About It

Think about how you could use body language to send each of the following messages. Describe the body language in the space provided.

1.    "I'm bored."

2.    "You are very interesting."

3.    "I'm happy to see you."

4.    "I'm afraid."

5.    "I'm proud of myself."

6.    "You make me nervous."

7.    "I don't like this."

8.    "I'm listening to you."

9.    "I'm sad about something."

10.    "I love you."

## Think About It

Suppose you really wanted to get to know someone. One day, you finally get up the nerve to talk to the person. You go up to the person. You introduce yourself. You tell the person that you've been wanting to talk to him for a long time. The person looks at you briefly. As he says, "Nice to meet you," he looks over his shoulder at someone else.

How would this communication make you feel? What message would you hear from the person's words? What message would you hear from the person's body language? Answer these questions in the space provided.

## Reviewing Unit 4: It's How You Say It

In Unit 4 you discovered that carefully choosing your words can help you reach your communication goal. You discovered words that help communication. You discovered words that harm communication.

Think about these things. Look back at Unit 4. Then work through the following activities. They will strengthen the skills you developed in Unit 4.

## Think About It

(Check your answers on page 123.)

1. Explain why good communicators choose their words carefully before speaking.

**2.** What are four types of words that good communicators avoid when sending a message?

## Think About It

Read each statement. Put a **+** next to the statements that contain words that help communication. Put a **−** next to the statements that contain words that harm communication. (Check your answers on page 123.)

_____ **1.** "I knew you'd get this all messed up! You never do anything right."

_____ **2.** "You fool! How could you have done such a stupid thing?"

_____ **3.** "Sometimes I feel as if you aren't listening to me."

_____ **4.** "I understand how you feel. I feel that way, too."

_____ **5.** "I'd like to talk to you about something."

_____ **6.** "I can't believe that you did that! How could you have been so dumb?"

_____ **7.** "We always have to do whatever you want!"

_____ **8.** "You are never happy anymore."

_____ **9.** "I'm not sure what you mean. Could you explain it to me again?"

_____ **10.** "We are doing whatever I say!"

## Think About It

Good communicators avoid using _you_ statements. Instead, good communicators use _I_ statements. Practice being a good communicator. Change each _you_ statement below to an _I_ statement.

**1.** "You don't pay any attention to me."

2. "You always choose the program we watch."

3. "You never help out around this apartment."

4. "You can't be serious about anything."

5. "You don't understand this at all."

6. "You think everything I say is stupid."

7. "You never act in a responsible manner."

8. "You always let me down."

## Reviewing Unit 5: Listen Carefully

In Unit 5 you discovered that listening is a part of communication. You learned how to develop a good listening attitude. You explored ways of showing a person that you are listening.

Think about these things. Look back at Unit 5. Then work through the following activities. They will strengthen the skills you developed in Unit 5.

## Think About It

Use your own words to explain the relationship between communication and listening. (Check your answers on page 123.)

## Check What You've Learned

Read each statement. Put a check mark next to the statements that show a good listening attitude. (Check your answers on page 123.)

\_\_\_\_ **1.** "I'm going to listen to everything she has to say."

\_\_\_\_ **2.** "If he starts yelling, I'm going to walk away."

\_\_\_\_ **3.** "I don't know why I'm even bothering to talk to this person."

\_\_\_\_ **4.** "I know that we can work this problem out."

\_\_\_\_ **5.** "I will ask her to explain how she feels about this situation."

\_\_\_\_ **6.** "Talking to her is like talking to a brick wall."

\_\_\_\_ **7.** "I'm not leaving until we find out what the problem is."

\_\_\_\_ **8.** "I know that we are going to end up having a fight."

\_\_\_\_ **9.** "I intend to pay close attention to everything she says."

\_\_\_\_ **10.** "I know that we can help each other out."

## Think About It

Explain three different things you can do to show a person that you are listening. (Check your answers on page 123.)

# Reviewing Unit 6: Put Yourself in Their Shoes

In Unit 6 you learned about point of view. You looked at different events from different points of view. You discovered that understanding another person's point of view helps resolve conflicts.

Think about these things. Look back at Unit 6. Then work through the following activities. They will strengthen the skills you developed in Unit 6.

## Think About It

(Check your answers on page 123.)

1. Use your own words to explain what point of view is. Write your answer in the space provided.

2. List the five steps to follow when trying to resolve a conflict.

## What About You?

Think about the last time you had a conflict with someone else. Then think about the five-step plan for solving conflicts. Describe how you could have used this plan to reach a solution. Go through each step of the plan.

# BOOK REVIEW

## Key Words

Match each word in Column A with the correct meaning in Column B. Write the letter from Column B on the answer blank in Column A. (Check your answers on page 123.)

**Column A**

_____ **1.** assume

_____ **2.** attitude

_____ **3.** body language

_____ **4.** communication

_____ **5.** conflict

_____ **6.** conversation

_____ **7.** emotion

_____ **8.** express oneself

_____ **9.** goal

_____ **10.** interpret

_____ **11.** messag

_____ **12.** negative

_____ **13.** point of view

_____ **14.** positive

**Column B**

**a.** harmful

**b.** to explain the meaning of something

**c.** purpose

**d.** healthy

**e.** an idea or information

**f.** the messages that your body sends to others

**g.** spoken exchange of ideas

**h.** strong feeling

**i.** sharing of ideas

**j.** to take something for granted

**l.** a person's way of acting, thinking, or feeling

**m.** the way a person thinks about people or events

**n.** to state one's thoughts or feelings

# Key Ideas

(Check your answers on page 123.)

1. What three things are needed in order for communication to happen?

2. Name six reasons people communicate.

3. What makes up your communication style?

4. Why do people have different communication styles?

5. Describe two types of body language and the message sent by each.

6. Why should a speaker's body language and message match?

7. Why do good communicators carefully choose their words?

8. What are four kinds of words that harm communication?

9. What are two kinds of words that help communication?

10. Explain the relationship between listening and communication.

11. Describe a good listening attitude.

12. What are two ways to show a speaker that you are listening?

13. Do all people share the same point of view? Explain why.

14. List the five steps in the plan for solving conflicts.

## What About You? _____

How has working through this book helped your communication skills?

# GLOSSARY

**assume:** to take something for granted, 76

**attitude:** a person's way of acting, thinking, or feeling, 76

**body language:** the messages that your body sends to others, 36

**communication:** the sharing of ideas, 4

**conflict:** disagreement, 95

**conversation:** a spoken exchange of ideas, 50

**emotion:** strong feeling, 22

**express oneself:** to state one's thoughts or feelings, 53

**goal:** purpose, 8

**interpret:** to explain the meaning of a message, 6

**message:** an idea or information, 4

**negative:** harmful, 11

**point of view:** the way a person thinks about people or events, 90

**positive:** healthy, 11

# ANSWER KEY

## Unit 1: Getting the Message Across

**Think About It** (p. 3)
1. c    2. a

**Think About It** (p. 4)
3

**Think About It** (p. 5)
Answers will vary but may include:
1. Hello; Glad to meet you
2. Go
3. Children in the area
4. Good; Yes
5. I'm married

**Check What You've Learned** (pp. 6-7)
1. Gaynelle; I went to the post office; husband
2. Masako; Concert was good; musicians
3. Ali; time out; referee
4. Cigarette company; Attractive people smoke; reader
5. Tom; I'm bored; wife
6. Counselor; I care, it's OK; Dawn
7. Son; I'm enjoying this show; Alicia
8. Parole officer; I'm angry; Bill
9. T    10. T    11. F    12. T    13. F

**Check What You've Learned** (p. 9)
1. To get to know someone
2. To learn
3. To have fun
4. To learn
5. To teach
6. To let someone know how you feel

**Check What You've Learned** (p. 10)
1. T    2. F    3. T

**Think About It** (p. 12)
1. Could you explain that again?
2. I need to be on time for my appointment.
3. Do you think I could choose what we will do today?
4. Could you let me pass?
5. Could you slow down a little?
6. I'd like to do something different today.
7. I'd love to hear how you feel about this.
8. Is everything OK?

## Unit 1 Review

**Key Words** (p. 14)
1. c    2. d    3. a    4. e    5. f    6. b

**Key Ideas** (p. 14)
1. There must be a sender, a message, and a receiver.
2. A message can be sent through actions, signs, or symbols.
3. People communicate to share ideas.
4. You can identify your communication goal, choose your words carefully, be honest, speak in a respectful way.
5. Negative practices cause the listener to stop hearing the sender's message.

## Unit 2: A Matter of Style

**Think About It** (p. 17)
No. They used negative body language and poor word selection.

**Think About It** (p. 22)
1. I would think that the person cared about me.
2. I would think that the person was bored and uninterested in me.

**Check What You've Learned** (p. 22)
1. F    2. T    3. T

**Check What You've Learned** (p. 27)
1. T    2. T    3. T    4. F    5. F

## Unit 2 Review

**Key Word** (p. 28)
strong feelings

**Key Ideas** (pp. 28–29)
1. Your communication style is made up of your tone of voice, background, body movements, gestures, and words.
2. Matching tone of voice to words helps a listener interpret a message.
3. A good communicator gets his message across, thinks about the listener, sends a clear message, shows that he values and respects the listener.
4. People have different opinions about eye contact, personal space, being direct, and time.

**5.** They feel it shows disrespect.

## Real-World Connection: The Job Interview

**Key Words** (p. 32)
**1.** b    **2.** d    **3.** a    **4.** d    **5.** b    **6.** d
**7.** a    **8.** d

**Check What You've Learned** (pp. 32-33)
**1.** c    **2.** d    **3.** b    **4.** d    **5.** a    **6.** c
**7.** b    **8.** a

**Think About It** (p. 33)
1. Gian's lack of eye contact made Mrs. Will think that he was not interested in the job.
2. No. Gian and Mrs. Will had different communication styles. Gian's style was indirect and Mrs. Will's style was direct.

## Unit 3: You Can't Hear It

**Think About It** (p. 35)
**1.** angry    **2.** uncomfortable

**Think About It** (p. 36)
Answers will vary, but may include angry, rude, tired, or cranky.

**Think About It** (p. 37)
Her body language hurt communication because it showed Ling that Mia didn't want to be bothered with her.

**Check What You've Learned** (p. 37)
**1.** T    **2.** F    **3.** F    **4.** T    **5.** T

**Think About It** (p. 38)
Answers will vary but may include:
1. The person is happy.
2. The person is sad or angry.
3. The person is very excited.
4. The person means what he says.
5. The person is bored or tired.
6. The person is annoyed.
7. The person means business.
8. The person is tired.
9. The person finds me attractive.
10. The person finds me interesting.
11. The person is annoyed.
12. The person is angry.

**Check What You've Learned** (p. 41)
**1.** F    **2.** T    **3.** T

**Check What You've Learned** (p. 45)
**1.** T    **2.** T    **3.** T

## Unit 3 Review

**Key Word** (p. 46)
using your body to send messages to others

**Key Ideas** (pp. 46-47)
1. Messages from body language are often more powerful that word messages.
2. Body language and words should match to help the listener interpret the message.
3. Examples of positive body language include: smiling, sitting up straight, looking directly at the listener, nodding your head as you talk.
4. Examples of negative body language include: frowning, yawning, pointing your finger, shaking your fist.
5. No. Actions can be interpreted in different ways.
6. To reach your goal, match words and body language.

## Unit 4: It's How You Say It

**Think About It** (p. 49)
They are arguing about which movie to attend.

**Think About It** (p. 51)
A low, serious tone of voice would have been better.

**Check What You've Learned** (p. 53)
**1.** thrilled    **2.** exhausted    **3.** gigantic
**4.** furious    **5.** miserable

**Check What You've Learned** (p. 54)
**1.** T    **2.** T    **3.** F    **4.** F    **5.** T

**Check What You've Learned** (pp. 57-58)
1. That hairstyle is very fashionable. But, I'm not sure that it shows off the curl in your hair.
2. Are you sure you want to move there? Did you think about how you would feel in that neighborhood?
3. Is everything all right?
4. I know this is hard to learn. It took me awhile to get the hang of it.
5. I'm not sure I understand what you mean.
6. I'm not sure that outfit shows off your figure.

**Think About It** (p. 59)
1, 4, 5, 7, 8, 10, 11, 12

**Check What You've Learned** (p. 59)
**1.** T    **2.** F    **3.** F    **4.** T    **5.** T

**Check What You've Learned** (p. 61)
Answers will vary but may include:
1. I feel like you're not listening to me.
2. I'd like it if you'd think about me sometimes.

**Check What You've Learned** (p. 63)
Answers will vary but may include:
1. I often feel that you aren't thinking about me.
2. I often feel as though I'm the only one who takes out the garbage.
3. I'd like it if you would help me with the chores sometimes.
4. You often forget to pick your clothes up off the floor.
5. It seems like I often have to answer the phone.

**Check What You've Learned** (p. 63)

1. F    2. T    3. T

# Unit 4 Review

**Key Words** (p. 64)
1. a spoken exchange of ideas
2. to state one's thoughts or feelings

**Key Ideas** (pp. 64-65)
1. You should think in order to send a clear message.
2. Answers will vary.
3. They send the message that change is impossible.
4. Answers will vary.
5. *I* messages explain how you feel, help the listener interpret the message, and don't blame the listener.

# Real-World Connection: The Phone Call

**Key Words** (p. 68)
1. b    2. d    3. c    4. d    5. b
6. c    7. a    8. b    9. c    10. d

**Check What You've Learned** (p. 69)
1. c    2. d    3. a    4. d    5. c
6. b    7. a    8. b    9. b    10. c

# Unit 5: Listen Carefully

**Think About It** (p. 72)
1. They are arguing about which show to watch.

2. Chico's favorite team is trying to win the championship.
3. It's Al's favorite program.

**Check What You've Learned** (p.75)
1. T    2. F    3. T

**Think About It** (p. 77)
It's likely that the men would have been able to work things out.

**Check What You've Learned** (pp. 77-78)
1. -    2. +    3. +    4. +    5. -    6. -
7. +    8. -    9. -    10. +    11. -    12. -
13. -    14. +    15. +

**Think About It** (pp. 80-81)
1. Miko is making an assumption and not keeping his emotions under control. Suggestions will vary.
2. Chuck did not treat Ryan in a respectful manner. Suggestions will vary.
3. Rhea is not keeping her emotions under control. Suggestions will vary.
4. Alex is not changing his communication goal. Suggestions will vary.

**Check What You've Learned** (p. 81
1. T    2. T    3. F    4. F    5. T

**Check What You've Learned** (p. 82)
1, 4, 5, 7, 8, 10

**Check What You've Learned** (p. 84)
1. T    2. T    3. F

# Unit 5 Review

**Key Words** (p. 85)
1. a person's way of acting, thinking, or feeling
2. to take something for granted

**Key Ideas** (pp. 85–86)
1. No. For communication to happen, there must be a sender, a message, and a receiver.
2. You should approach the communication in a positive way.
3. Treat others with respect, be willing to change your communication goals, don't make assumptions, keep emotions under control
4. Making an assumption stops the listener from hearing the message.
5. It shows that you've heard the message and interpreted it.

6. Nod your head, make eye contact, sit straight or stand tall.

7. You can show understanding by restating the speaker's words exactly or in your own words.

8. Listening carefully shows the speaker that you respect his thoughts and feelings. It helps you understand the listener's point of view, which aids in resolving conflict.

## Unit 6: Put Yourself In Their Shoes

**Think About It** (p. 89)

1. c    2. b

**Think About It** (p. 90)

No. Each person is a unique individual with different life experiences.

**Think About It** (pp. 92-93)

1. **Problem:** Ike wants to borrow Tim's car but Tim doesn't want to lend it to him. **Ike's Point of View:** I need to borrow the car in order to take out someone that I really like. **Tim's Point of View:** I just got my car and I'm really proud of it. I don't know if Ike will take care of it the way I do.

2. **Problem:** Kay wants Joe to attend a party but he doesn't want to go. **Kay's Point of View:** I really like Joe. I want my friends to get to know him. **Joe's Point of View:** I don't like parties. They make me feel uncomfortable. I really don't want to go to a party where I am the new person.

3. **Problem:** Mike wants a dog but Bud does not want a pet. **Mike's Point of View:** I really love dogs. I will take care of the dog and pay for everything. It won't affect Bud at all. **Bud's Point of View:** I don't like pets. I don't want an animal ruining the apartment.

**Check What You've Learned** (p. 94)

1. F    2. T    3. T    4. F    5. T

**Check What You've Learned** (pp. 98-99)

1. 4, 1, 5, 3, 2    2. T    3. T    4. F
5. T    6. T

## Unit 6 Review

**Key Words** (p. 100)

1. the way a person thinks about people or events.

2. a disagreement

**Key Ideas** (pp. 100–101)

1. People have different points of view because of their various backgrounds and life experiences.

2. Think about the person and his or her life.

3. Name the problem, see both points of view, list possible solutions, examine the list, find the best solution.

4. A good solution is one that suits both sides.

5. *Agree to disagree* means that you decide that the problem cannot be worked out and that you will respect each side's opinion.

## Unit 7: Put It Into Practice

**Think About It** (p. 103)

Communication is the sharing of ideas.

**Check What You've Learned** (pp. 104–105)

1. Sender: Sean; Message: I can't go to the store; Receiver: Ryan

2. Sender: Pat; Message: I had an accident; Receiver: Carl

3. Sender: Jim; Message: I have two tickets to tonight's baseball game; Receiver: Mark

4. Sender: Eva; Message: I was up all night; Receiver: Zoe

**Think About It** (p. 105)

1. A communication goal is what you want to achieve or your purpose.

2. To let someone know how you feel, to get to know someone, to teach or share information, to learn, to entertain or have fun, to solve a problem

3. Carefully choose your words, be honest, speak in a respectful way

**Check What You've Learned** (pp. 105–106)

1. I'm not sure I understand what you mean.

2. I understand why you feel that way. But, I feel differently.

3. I would not want to do that.

4. I don't think you have all the facts straight.

5. I'd appreciate it if you would try to do what I ask.

6. I would really enjoy hearing how you feel about this.

7. I'm not sure that outfit suits you.

8. It would make me happy to choose the movie tonight.

9. Sometimes I feel as if you don't listen to me.
10. I'd like to be on time tonight.

**Think About It** (p. 107)
1. Communication style is the way you send messages.
2. Your communication style includes your tone of voice, background, body movements and gestures, and words.
3. Strong emotions can harm communication. They can make a listener stop hearing a message.

**4–8.** Answers will vary.

**Check What You've Learned**
(pp. 107–108)
1. F    2. T    3. T    4. F    5. T

**Think About It** (p. 108)
Body language is how you use your body to send messages.

**Think About It** (pp.110–111)
1. Good communicators choose their words carefully to clearly express their thoughts and feelings in a way that the listener will understand.
2. Good communicators avoid using words that blame or criticize, using the words *always* and *never* when criticizing, and calling people names.

**Check What You've Learned** (p. 111)
1. -    2. -    3. +    4. +    5. +
6. -    7. -    8. -    9. +    10. -

**Think About It** (p. 113)
In order for communication to happen, listening must take place.

**Check What You've Learned** (p. 113)
1, 4, 5, 7, 9, 10

**Think About It** (p. 113)
To show a person that you're listening, you could nod your head, make eye contact, sit up straight, or restate the speaker's words either directly or in your own words.

**Think About It** (p. 114)
1. Point of view is the way a person thinks about people or events.
2. The five steps to resolve a conflict are:

name the problem, see both points of view, list possible solutions, examine the list, find the best solution.

# Book Review

**Key Words** (p. 115)
1. j    2. l    3. f    4. i    5. k    6. g
7. h    8. n    9. c    10. b    11. e
12. a    13. m    14. d

**Key Ideas** (pp. 116-117)
1. The three things needed for communication are a sender, a message, and a receiver.
2. People communicate to let someone know how they feel, to get to know someone, to teach or share information, to learn, to entertain or have fun, and to solve a problem.
3. Your words, background, tone of voice, body movements, and gestures make up your communication style.
4. Each person has different backgrounds and life experiences.
5. Answers will vary.
6. Body language and messages should match to help a listener interpret the communication
7. Good communicators choose words that clearly state their thoughts and feelings.
8. Four kinds of words that harm communication are: words that blame, criticize, call people names, and *always* and *never* when criticizing.
9. *I* messages, using the words *often* and *sometimes*, help communication.
10. Listening is part of communication.
11. A good listening attitude shows respect for the speaker.
12. To show a speaker that you're listening, nod your head, make eye contact, sit up straight, and restate what the speaker said.
13. No. This is caused by differences in life experiences.
14. The five steps for solving conflicts include: name the problem, see both points of view, list possible solutions, examine the list, and find the solution.

# PHOTO CREDITS